HITTING *the* WALL

Winning the game of business by breaking through your own barriers

Proofreading and editing: Writers Ink
Cover design, interior layout and book publishing:
Plum Design & Publishing Ltd - www.plumdesignpublishing.com

ISBN: 978-1-8382608-0-4

Published in November 2020 by the Business Clubhouse Ltd in collaboration with Plum Design & Publishing Ltd and The Business Ghost

www.thebusinessclubhouse.co.uk

This book would not exist without the love and support of the most incredible people anyone could wish to have in their life:

Mum - Thank you for everything

Rabbit - You'll always be my reason

Kay - My rock and my safe harbour

Dad - I know you're proud of me

Seema - Sleep well x

Matt,

Best wishes

Ash

WHAT OTHERS SAY

"What Ash has managed to do with this book you are holding is distil a life of questions, discovery and learning into something quite special. I challenge anyone to read Hitting The Wall and not come away with more focus, clarity and understanding. Understanding of yourself and what you are trying to achieve.

As Pink Floyd told us in some style in 1979, we build our walls ourselves, and we allow the people around us to pass us one brick after another. It is time you starting building ones that lift you higher, or break down the walls that hold you back.

If you are standing in a bookshop, still deciding if you should pick up this book and read it, then I have only one question for you: What could you gain from it?

If you've already made the decision, get on with it! Read carefully though, the questions you really need to answer are not always that obvious. You have to dig for them a bit.

Enjoy your quest."

Pieter K de Villiers

Co-founder and Chief Product Officer, Macanta
Author of '*Barefoot Business*' & Co-author of '*Franchise Freedom*'

"An honest, creative and thought-provoking read regardless of your industry. If you are looking for structures, methods or just some new perspective to get you on the path to achieving your next goal, this will give you exactly that so that you can break down your barriers – and use the walls to climb over or support you."

Dave Pearman - Shopping Centre Manager

....

"I've read many business books, but none have grabbed my attention like Ash's. He writes in a way that is really accessible and inspirational, combining good advice and motivational exercises with insight into his own successes and failures. Highly recommended, read it!"

Jane Stewart - Chief Executive Basingstoke Together BID

....

"If you're a small business owner, you've no doubt had your struggles. What Ash does in this book is to help you understand that it's all about what goes on between your ears. Through personal experiences laid bare, he skillfully deals with the "head trash" that we all have and helps to move you on so you can focus on the important stuff.

I encourage anyone with even a hint of an open mind to have a read... and I'd wager a hefty sum that you'll find some nuggets in there that will really make a difference."

John Thompson - Your Next Mortgage & JEDZ Bottles

....

"When Ash said he was going to write a book, I couldn't wait to read it. We've been friends for ages, and he has helped me a lot – but I just knew there would be more to understand and learn about him, his past experience and his knowledge. I thoroughly enjoyed it!"

Marie Haywood - Five Star Furnishing Care

"Ash's love for tennis translates to so many useful lessons in business because, like in sports, you get back what you put in. And, the repetitive process of hitting a tennis ball against a wall Ash has described in this book is a brilliant reminder that keeping things simple is the key to success.

Reading the book, then breaking down the six lessons in each chapter, offers insightful observations on the processes you need to take. I've learned a lot from my first read, and I know it's one I will read again and again."

Robbie Richardson - Richardson & Paige, Upholsterers of Distinction

....

"Ash shares his own rich, personal, and potentially devastating experiences of life and business in this book. I can identify with him because juggling family life while also starting then running my business has not always been easy. Understanding the walls Ash has bumped into on his journey helped me recognise my walls. Mine may not be as big, but can still feel either impossible to scale on my own or are piles of rubble that continually trip me up. The six lessons in each chapter are easy to understand and relate to everyday life. Each one makes me think not just about business, but how my life works as a whole.

I know I will be coming back to them over and over again, and I really appreciate the truth and honesty of Ash's story. I look forward to hearing more from him."

Carole Simpson - Keep Phytt

FOREWORD

There are times in life when you get to do something that just makes you smile from ear to ear.

Writing this foreword is one of them.

I've known Ash for nearly ten years. Our paths first crossed at an event in Bracknell, Berkshire shortly after I'd just bought into a regional business and one of the clients of the new business networking/mentoring group was Ash Taylor Tennis. To be honest, I was a little worried about meeting the owner as his reputation in this business circle of owners was legendary.

I asked a few people who this Ash Taylor was, and was directed to a group of people at the bar. There was one character who was holding court, everyone hanging on his every word. Yes, this was Ash.

I approached with a slight pang of nerves and introduced myself, explaining that I was the new Business Growth Manager for the Thames Valley area, and would love to chat to him at some point on how we could help him.

What surprised me was the reception I got. Yes, this person was revered and could have easily believed in the hype that was presented to him, but what I saw then, and still do to this day, was a fun-loving, caring person who could not do enough to help people who had a genuine need.

As you will learn from this book, Ash had taken a job and created a business that went from £30k to £300k in just a few short months. In this circle he was living the dream. He was part of a high-level Mastermind

Group that you had to be invited into. He had created a marketing machine that was inspired and had spawned lots of imitators (detailed in **Chapter Four, Lesson Six: You cannot teach tennis from a book**).

My own personal journey through the business world has been varied: selling my own business in my late twenties, my CEO days in charge of a nine-figure business in my thirties, through to coaching clients and helping run Mastermind Groups throughout my forties. As you can imagine, I have met many accomplished business people during those times, but what I recognised in Ash was a person that was able to take his real-life experiences and relate them as practical business lessons to business owners. My coaching is based on the business, and the needs of the business. Ash discovered that his experiences and understanding of them really related to the business owner.

There comes a time in life when certain roads meet and something special happens. For Ash this was December 2013. His tennis business had served up its last lesson due to lots of factors (see **Chapter Four: Running Blind**) and he was explaining this to my Mastermind Group and trying to figure out what he would do next. That one session provided Ash with not only the answers but also the vehicle going forward.

Ash was, is, and will always be a people person. His innate skill is to help people see what they need to do, whether it is on a tennis court, as a friend, or as a business owner coach. What emerged that Mastermind day was Ash's realisation that people looked up to him for his understanding of them as a business owner, the trials and tribulations they encounter, and the tools and support they needed to help them run their business.

I've learned a lot from Ash, but the most important thing was his ability to focus on and help others, even if he was personally suffering at the time.

Right now, you have in your hands, thirty great experiences and the lessons learned, told by one of life's true givers. Whether that was from his experience on a tennis court, his personal tragedies and how that impacted him, his various roles in life as a business owner and father, his highs and lows as an Entrepreneur, and how it's okay to not to be perfect but to find ways to continue.

I count myself VERY fortunate to have met Ash through business, get closer to him, become a mentor, close friend, attend his stag do in Budapest (another story) and his wedding to Kay. You may not be as fortunate as me to meet him, but reading this book will give you a taste of what he offers...

Martin Norbury

Investor, Mentor, Entrepreneur
Author of '*I don't work Fridays*'

CONTENTS

*"See that guy there in the mirror?
That's the toughest opponent you're
ever going to have to face"*

Rocky Balboa

INTRODUCTION

You, me and the wall

Travel five miles slightly east of north, in a dead straight line, from the world-famous All England Lawn Tennis and Croquet Club (aka Wimbledon) and you'll arrive at a lesser-known tennis coaching establishment. Number Nine, Aubrey Walk, W8 is the home of Campden Hill Lawn Tennis Club, and that building shaped my life. Well, not the exact building that stands there today, but on the same foundation of the club's new headquarters there once stood a wall. It was nondescript, to say the least, and I may be the only person alive who even remembers that it once occupied the space. And I am certain I'm the only one who could describe every scratch, chip, discoloured brick and the crack that decorated its breadth about three feet from the floor.

This story begins with my trek from Aubrey Walk to a career in coaching and the wall that took me there. But, of course, none of life's journeys consist of a dead straight line. And not even the convoluted maze of London's traffic bound, diversionary and illogical, stop-start routes from one place to another can describe the true nature of the battles we face along our way. To describe life as a journey suggests there is always a way to find, or a predestined path is laid out for each one of us. But that is not true. If everything happens for a reason, what about people whose lives are cut short or the ones who are born to, live through, then die in abstract poverty? How did that reason help them?

The reality is that life is a mixture of chance, choices, open doors and cold, hard, unfeeling, immovable brick walls. And the only way to break through is learning to seize opportunities and use those same walls to your advantage. In the pages that follow, I hope to show you how I do that and, more importantly, how you can achieve the same.

This book is also about running a business – but not about the business itself. Let me explain. Throughout my time as a tennis coach, I never once taught a ball how to cross the net and bounce just inside the baseline. Nor did I ever train a racket to deliver a wicked slice causing the ball to spin away from an opponent on impact. I only ever coached the person who held the racket or hit that ball.

And business success is just the same. Identifying and then refining your rhythm, reasons, and perfect swing (as a business owner) is the only way to ensure you achieve the results your effort deserves.

Five sets and thirty thoughts.

Hitting the Wall describes five significant events in my life and some of the lessons, thoughts and life-changing moments those events taught me.

My big hope is that you, and if not you then just one person who reads this story, will learn how to turn their walls into milestones.

Enjoy.

Ash Taylor

1

THE WALL

Enemy, friend, tormentor and coach

One, two, three, four, five, miss... another false start in a skinny, nervous, untalented, yet determined kid's quest to master the magic twenty. As an eleven-year-old boy, I was frightened of everything and everyone. I was the smallest boy at school, and even most of the girls had more weight behind their shoves and punches than me. So, my early years at Holland Park School were spent running away from the first sight of trouble and the final bell of the day. When I got home, however, everything changed. I became Stefan Edberg beating Boris Becker at Wimbledon – in my imagination at least. There was nothing about my frame to suggest I would be good at sports, especially such a physically demanding activity like tennis. And my track record at school confirmed the outward appearance. Like muscles, it seemed, natural talent had passed me by, and I excelled in nothing. But there was something about hitting that tatty old tennis ball against the office wall of the Campden Hill Lawn Tennis Club in Aubrey Walk that captured my attention. And before long it caught someone else's attention too.

The tennis club was at number nine, and I lived with my parents and my younger sister, Seema, at number seven Aubrey Walk. Don't think for a moment that because we lived next door to a tennis club, with a W8 postcode, it meant we could afford to join. If you know anything about London, at all, you'll understand how space compels the rich and the poor to live as neighbours as they often share a pavement. But I could afford to hit a faded yellow tennis ball against an Edwardian wall with my heavy wooden racket whenever I escaped school and my chores.

So, there I was one day, striving to smash my rally record of seventeen when a tall man in a smart tracksuit stopped and asked my name. I'd seen him walking by many times before and entering the club so, in my mind, he wasn't one of those strangers us kids were always being warned not to talk to. I told him it was Ash. He then introduced himself as Peter and said he worked at the club. The next day, just as I was about to serve out the final game in the Wimbledon semi-final, Peter stopped again and asked, "How many do you think you can hit today, Ash?"

"Maybe forty or fifty?" I replied, nervous about looking like a complete no-hoper.

"How about aiming for twenty-five?" Peter said with a smile before walking through the club doors to work with some of the brightest young talent London had to offer the world of racket sports. Peter Henesey Smith was the Head Coach of Campden Hill Lawn Tennis Club, and, if the wall and everything that it came to stand for changed my life, Peter ensured it was a change for the better. You see, walls can stop you in your tracks or direct you towards a different horizon – which way you go often depends on whose voice you choose to listen to.

In the months and years that followed, helped by Peter's challenges and occasional coaching, my rallies soared way beyond seventeen. At the point where most serves, except for the ones interrupted by passing cars, advanced to triple figures, the numbers became less relevant to me. The joy of returning the ball, time and time again, overtook the need for a number; and the practice, persistence and hard yards of striving for perfection became my new horizon. Along the way, my 'off-court' life changed for the better too. I held my head higher at school; the bullying lessened and finally stopped, and I started earning money by grafting on local lawns, washing cars, emptying lofts and any other commercial venture I could find. The wall I'd sometimes hated for sending me an extra-wide return had become a friend helping to explore and expand my limits.

On my thirteenth birthday, there I was hitting my ball against the club office wall. Two hundred and twenty-one, two twenty-two, two twenty-three... "Hey Ash," Peter interrupted my flow, "can you come up to the office for a few minutes?" I was no stranger to the club by then and had occasionally been invited in to play on the courts at quieter times of the week or weekends – but this sounded formal. My mind rushing for a reason, I recalled the window I had broken the week before and wondered how they knew it was me. When I got to the clubhouse bar, Ingrid the club's manager was there, along with Hugh Levington, Al Hill and Peter. Looking from face to face, no one was giving anything away, although I thought I detected a smile from Al. When I was handed a brown paper envelope, I pondered how many washed cars it would take to cover the bill.

Inside the envelope was a brand-new membership card with my name on it: Ash Taylor, Junior Member of Campden Hill Lawn Tennis Club, Season 1983-84.

I learned later that Peter had called an Extraordinary General Meeting, where he had threatened to leave the club unless the local children were given a way to join. For the first time in the club's one-hundred-year history, juniors who were not children of existing members could join and train with professional coaches. More than that, though, it turned out that Peter had paid for my membership out of his own pocket. He asked me to spread the word that membership fees had been reduced from £200 to £20 per week for children in the local community. Over the next few weeks, my popularity around the neighbourhood grew, as I happily accepted credit for opening the club's doors to anyone who cared.

To my shame (I was thirteen and thrilled to bits at the time) it was not until many years later that I remembered to ask Peter why he had chosen to help me. His answer was instant and simple, and it stopped me in my tracks. "You never gave up," he said. And it was shortly after that, during a slightly inebriated and impromptu speech at his wedding, that I finally owned up to smashing the window. Of course, he already knew, but that hadn't stopped him putting his faith in me (or threatening to send me the bill).

I didn't know it at the time, but from the first day Peter had asked my name and challenged me to hit a number – any number would have done – he became the second coach in my life. The first one was the wall itself. You see, every single time it returned the ball to me, whether it was straight onto my racket, or one I had to chase across the road, I got a little bit better. The margins were indecipherably small, but not a single shot was wasted; because I was consistent in my effort, and the wall was always there. From hitting the wall outside of Campden Hill Lawn Tennis Club, I went on to work alongside Peter and the other coaches inside the club walls. After leaving school with an average education, I progressed to coaching roles at other clubs and eventually working for the Lawn Tennis Association (the national governing body for tennis in the UK). I represented my club in tournaments all over the country, even playing on the hallowed Wimbledon courts, and had a few memorable shots at breaking through. But I was always going to be a better coach than I was a player of the sport. And while I might still occasionally awake with the Wimbledon trophy within my grasp, it is more likely to be the Ryder Cup that occupies my 'what could have been' moments these days.

This is a book about lessons from walls, capturing moments and moving forward. And, as I leave the story of my first wall experience here, let me introduce you to the format for this chapter and the rest of the book. The following six parts will highlight lessons you can learn from hitting balls against the walls in your life and practical steps you can take to apply them. Each of the subsequent chapters will follow the same pattern: a summary of a different wall encounter and six steps towards making a difference in your life.

Enjoy the game and I hope you win in the end.

LESSON ONE

Practice makes permanent

The saying 'practice makes perfect' is so misleading it sends shivers down my spine every time I hear its deceptive tone. It simply is not true. Imagine an apprentice carpenter cuts his finger while chiselling towards the hand that is holding the wood. Does the expert tell him to keep practising? Or does he correct his technique, showing him how to use a clasp and point the sharp end away from his body and hands? The late great Jim Rohn summed it up when he wrote, 'If someone is going down the wrong road, he doesn't need motivation to speed him up. What he needs is education to turn him around'.

The same thing happens all the time in business and is the cause of most business failures. People develop bad habits, especially in mindset and attitude. And their resistance to change or lack of education leads to a lifetime of poor practice and continual reinforcement of negative behaviours. The saddest thing about this cycle is that the harder someone tries, the worse they make it for themselves. Effort is only useful if it is applied in the right direction with the correct technique. That is not to say there is only one right way of doing things. Everyone is different, and one person's perfect practice of technique might not suit the next person. But what you repeatedly do must be effective for you, or it will rapidly become a bad habit and a hindrance to your success.

Later in the book, we will look at ways of measuring success and examining the actions you took to achieve it. By doing this continually, as a process, you will make incremental improvements in practice and outcome. But practice alone is only a means to the end or direction you are facing, for better or worse.

The road to success is boring

Surely there is no feeling on earth to compare with winning. Whether it is the football team whose colours run through your veins lifting the FA Cup; a big deal you've been working on for months finally getting to the 'signing on the dotted line' stage; or seeing your only child being born after the struggle of labour. Nothing beats that winning feeling. We revel in the moment of victory. We try and capture it in photographs, memorabilia, rewarding ourselves or reliving it in the days and years to come – but the precious moment itself is everything. Those moments are rare, and even more valuable for it, which is why we all long for success. But why are successes so important and so sought after? Because real success never comes cheaply. We work so damn hard to achieve it, seeing the effort pay off makes winning worthwhile. A gifted victory never seems to taste as sweet as a hard fought one.

The truth of the matter is that the work itself is rarely glamorous. Becoming great at something takes practice. Hours and hours of long and tedious, hitting a ball against a wall practice. It requires learning how to do something really well and repeatedly doing the same thing over and over again. The route to victory is boring, but it is the only way to get there. In the same way, it is easy to rattle off age-old platitudes like 'practice makes perfect' without ever examining the truth of the matter. It is human nature to ignore the necessity of the process. The next time you watch a top athlete revel in the glory of their gold medal moment, put aside that unworthy 'it could have been me' envy and picture their decades of sacrifice and graft.

Over those two or three years where Peter was stopping me in the street and challenging me to rally higher numbers in my quest to conquer the wall, he did more than just talk. He would stand there for a while and watch me hit the ball back. Then he would walk over and adjust my grip, nudge my feet slightly further apart or suggest another minor subtlety in my swing. He would set targets and tell me that when I could get to seventy-five, he would come and show me something else to improve my backhand. And remember, all this time, all I was doing was hitting a second-hand tennis ball against a battered old wall over and over, back and forth, to and fro, until my mum called me in for dinner. I could move up and down that wall, passing-cars permitting, and not miss a single return for ten minutes at a time before I'd even set foot on a tennis court (although in my head I was already a thirty-time Wimbledon Champion). So, when it came to facing my first real-life opponent – I was ready.

Is there something you could be better at in your business or life? Are you avoiding mastering a valuable skill because it is too hard, or you don't like it? I'm not talking about things you don't need to do (admin, bookkeeping, answering phones or fixing your IT), but attributes that would add to your life, make you happy or create opportunities to do the things you want to do. If those things are important to you, find a coach, take some lessons; and practise.

LESSON TWO

Talent is a myth: a dangerous one

If you have ever read any of Matthew Syed's beautiful books on sport, business and life achievement, you can pretty much skip this chapter. Matthew lived in a small town near Reading, Berkshire, and spent much of his time playing table tennis in the garage with his brother. Most of his friends, at school and down his street, had a similar obsession with table tennis and he a grew up assuming every child all over the world did the same.

Later in life, as he became three-time men's singles champion at the Commonwealth Table Tennis Championships and spent many years as the British Number One in the sport, he reflected on an oddity. Most of the people playing alongside him in the national team were also from Earley, a town with a population of less than 25,000 at the time. And some had even lived in the same street as his family. The more he thought about this coincidence it occurred to him that, as popular spectator sports go in the UK, his was some way behind football, cricket, rugby, golf, motor racing and even thrill-filled events like snooker and darts.

When he looked into this more, it turned out one of the volunteers at his school had coached at an international level, and several other enthusiastic players ran the local table tennis club. (How many UK towns even have a dedicated table tennis club, let alone people who are devoted to promoting the sport?) He started to understand that his upbringing, surrounded by table tennis, was pretty unique. Based on his observations of the geographical origins of Britain's table tennis elite, Syed started to form a theory. It is one of the foundation themes in many of his books, and it states that natural talent is not something anyone is born with. He digs deep into the backstories of an eclectic array of champions; from the obsessive parent of a chess-prodigy through to the distance running stars of small Kenyan villages who run twenty miles to school and back each day. And what he discovers is amazing – yet obvious when you stop and think about it. Talent is born where opportunity or necessity crosses the path of repeatedly or obsessively doing the same thing over and over again. Whether the activity is deliberate or accidental, if it is consistent and technically correct, the participant will eventually become a master. The wax-on, wax-off scene from the 80s classic Karate Kid comes to mind.

You can do anything you put your mind and effort to

It is easy to say you can achieve anything you put your mind to. In fact, saying anything is usually easier than doing it. But if you follow a proven methodology and you are committed to putting in the required hours of practice (the magical 10,000 hours is often cited for mastery) you are pretty much guaranteed to receive the title 'talented' at your graduation. There are some obvious caveats, of course: at four-foot-eleven-inches, you are never going to make it in the NBA or become Heavyweight Champion of the World, but the principle stands the test in every other respect.

The exciting thing for me, someone who works closely with business owners, is that the physical exceptions and limitations that might hinder sporting success are less relevant in life. And the age factor, being past your sporting best, can also be swept aside because we are focusing on mindset and activity. My experience, in parallel to the extensive research and case studies of people like Matthew Syed, is that anyone, at any stage of their working life, can work smarter, achieve more, and find the successful outcomes that fuel their dreams.

Lack of natural talent is no longer an excuse because natural talent has never been a real thing. The only thing stopping you is your belief in yourself and your willingness to apply yourself to action.

LESSON THREE

Vision boards

Alice: "Would you tell me, please, which way I ought to go from here?"

The Cheshire Cat: "That depends a good deal on where you want to get to."

Alice: "I don't much care where."

The Cheshire Cat: "Then it doesn't much matter which way you go."

That classic scene from Alice in Wonderland has long been written off as nothing more than an obscure encounter with a rather creepy fictional cat. Listen carefully, however, and you might just spot one of the most profound truths in the entire world of literature. You see, if you do not have a defined goal or direction, all of today's efforts are a waste of time. No, I am not talking about distant goals you need to work towards, regardless of today – I mean goals that make today worth living and move you towards future aspirations.

When I started hitting the ball against the wall of the tennis club, it was enjoyable and driven by a daydream – yet it was without purpose. But, as Peter stopped, challenged and focused my ambition, my process found direction and aim, and it began to mean something. With his guidance, I was able to build on hitting progressively higher numbers of returns; and to developing style, technique and capabilities that could win tennis matches. My training changed and adapted to each new element of the game Peter taught me.

You can apply the same idea to your business by identifying a goal and working out the steps you need to get you there. Then, you devise the practice, activities or processes required to fulfil each of the steps. It could be a financial target, a new product launch, developing a team to take the weight from your shoulders or learning an important new skill that will elevate you above your competition. All these things sound good, in principle, but you need to have a reason for wanting to achieve them, and a step plan in place to get you there.

This chapter is all about setting goals, and in it, I want to teach you how to create a vision board. Now, bear with me here, this is not a woo-woo, new-age gimmick – this is proven science.

Your brain cannot distinguish between things it wants and things it already has. It treats not having something you want the same as if you had lost a valued possession. Not having that thing causes tension that your brain seeks to resolve. The left hemisphere of your brain is a logical, detailed manager of time. It wants to know why, what, how and when. The right hemisphere exists in the sensory moment. It revels in the here and now, is intuitive, creative, and has no sense of time. It lives for experiences, and it wants them instantly. Creating a vision board will placate the conflict in your brain (that causes angst and unhappiness) and help you focus on the process instead.

I have been using this process myself for over ten years, and it works. The other secret the process reveals is identifying the steps you need to achieve your goals. And here is the most powerful thing of all – the goals the vision board will reveal for you are not a distant horizon, they are activities you can start today and enjoy for the rest of your life. There are three stages to creating your vision board, so let's get started.

Stage One: Unpackaging your goals

The hardest thing about setting goals and the reason people often fail to make a good job of it is that we don't stop long enough to work out what we *actually* want. The first stage of this process is designed to get everything out of your head and identify the most important things. Please, trust the process, and give it a try.

You will need:

- Ten sheets of A5 paper
- Three sheets of A4 paper
- One sheet of A3 paper
- A dozen different coloured pens/pencils
- A highlighter pen

Find a place away from distractions, put on your favourite music, and you are ready to start. Write the word **'Health'** in the middle of the first sheet of A5 paper. Then set a two-minute timer and write down every desire that comes into your mind regarding your **health, fitness and wellbeing.** Don't overthink it; just get everything out of your head.

When the two minutes are up, grab another A5 sheet, a different coloured pen, and repeat the exercise with each of these remaining topics:

- Wealth and financial planning
- Business goals
- Contribution or charity
- Spiritual or religious beliefs
- Family and home life
- Friends and social
- Education and learning
- Hobbies and other activities
- Anything else that matters in your life

Stage Two: Refining your goals

Now, go back through each sheet of paper, in turn, and highlight the things that stand out most. Maybe your subconscious has revealed a hidden desire, or even the act of writing something down reminded you of a forgotten gem you would love to see come true. Now list all the highlighted items on the A4 paper (you may need two or three sheets if your imagination went wild). As you transfer them across, feel free to refine, combine or expand your notions into defined activities or ambitions. You may find that ideas cross over between themes and sheets.

Grab your pen and narrow the list once more, highlighting the items on your list that capture your heart the most. These will be the ones that release a little bit of emotion or adrenaline as you read them and things that make your heart say, 'if only' or 'I actually think that is possible'. Stick to the ones that represent the most life-value to you today.

Stage Three: Process, action and vision

One at a time, take each target and write it on the A3 sheet of paper. And underneath, I want you to turn each goal into a SMART target, as follows:

- Specific: the idea is to persuade your brain that this is really happening
- Measurable: you need to be able to track your progress
- Achievable: ambitious is good (but impossible is not going to fool your brain)
- Relevant: these goals need to be driven by what *you* want (not other people)
- Timed: set a timescale or other measurements you can work towards

Turning a goal into a SMART target means your ambition to 'get fitter' might become 'I will be able to run 5k in less than 40 minutes by 31st August'. Another useful motivator would be to add two or three reasons the goal is important to you, alongside each target. For example 'I recently heard that heart disease runs in the family' or 'I need to fit into my best suit before my daughter's wedding'. The final piece of the written goal method is to translate your SMART target into the present tense. Tell your brain that you will achieve these outcomes by creating it in the here and now: 'It is 1st September, and I just ran 5k in 39 minutes'.

Another piece of astounding brain science suggests our brains interpret images in the same way they do real things. So, I want you to find pictures (yes, you can get a young person to help you) that represent each of these goals and decorate your written targets with the images. Make the pictures real, relevant and as accurate as possible, so that you ensure your brain believes you are going to achieve these goals. I turn my vision boards into screensavers as well as having physical copies attached to the fridge door and on the wall in the office.

As I said earlier, this is not a woo-woo idea; it is based on neuroscience, my personal experience and that of dozens of my clients. It is not exact though and will work better for different people and according to how much you commit to the method. But what I can absolutely guarantee is people who have a vision, and quantifiable targets, will always achieve more of their dreams, hopes and desires than those who don't – and you get to choose if that is what you want.

The final thought about vision boards I want to leave you with is, you should start taking proactive and positive action towards reaching those goals every day. The tiniest step in that direction will give you satisfaction today (because you will know you are winning) and will build momentum for every other positive thing in your life.

LESSON FOUR

Why tennis?

I have read a lot about neuroscience and why our brains work the way they do. It is a truly incredible study and shows how our subconscious is a far more powerful driver of our actions and choices than the more deliberate and conscious side of our intentions. When I think about the wall that became my childhood rallying partner for so many years, I wonder what career path I might have taken had I lived next door to a hockey club, football field or a swimming pool. As I stood there hitting ball after ball, watching coaches and smartly dressed players enter the club to play on finely cut, floodlit courts, my inner mind must have seen what the future could be. I certainly imagined being a Grand Slam champion, while battling the wall in my dreams at night and during idle classroom moments. Without knowing what I was doing, my mind had created a vision board, and my path through life seemingly took me there without my permission or the need to question its plan.

You may be surprised to know that I have not picked up a tennis racket or stepped foot on a court for over ten years. I only follow the tennis when Wimbledon is on, and even then, I would unquestioningly spend my time on cricket or my beloved QPR if I had to choose between the two. Today, my only participation sport is golf (and the associated gym work I have to put in to keep my handicap in check). I have pictures of me playing golf on my vision board; alongside clearly defined SMART targets declaring the improvements I will make in my game. I've stated by when and the resulting awards, trophies or personal achievements that will come about as a result. I have learned how to take control of the immense power within my subconscious mind, and I would urge you to do the same.

Here is an example of a SMART goal I set and achieved in my golf game. Yes, this might seem a little like self-indulgence, but I hope it will demonstrate why it is such a valuable thing for you to do in your life and business.

I want to become a better golfer

A general statement of intention like, 'I want to become a better golfer' is not going to help anyone achieve the result. For one thing, it doesn't even identify what a result would mean. That was, however, the sentence I first wrote on a piece of paper during a vision board exercise in August 2019. At the time, my *handicap was 20 and, after the refinement process described in the previous chapter, my desire translated into the following SMART statement:

'It is August 2020, and I am now playing off a handicap of 15'.

**Each hole on a golf course is given a par (the number of shots a professional golfer is expected to use to get the ball in the hole), which in turn provides a par for the entire (18-hole) course. A player's handicap is calculated using a simple algorithm to assess their ability in relation to their recent scorecards. For example, if your average score on a par-72 course is 84, you would be playing off a handicap of 12 (the difference). This means players with varying handicaps can go around in a group and still compete equally by applying their individual handicaps to their score.*

Having a clear and defined goal is incredibly powerful and focuses the mind. But it is the process that will take you to the destination. I set about assessing my current game, using various apps and technologies to measure the stronger and weaker areas of my play. It was no surprise to me to discover I was strong with long irons and putting, but my pitching and chipping were letting me down. In essence, I dropped shots most often when the ball fell 40 to 50 yards from the green, and I needed one shot to land it within putting distance.

I set myself some training exercises, both when practicing alone and when playing rounds with other people. Interestingly, that meant my game got worse before it got better because on some holes, I would deliberately send the ball short so I could practise a 50-yard pitch in a real-life situation. For six or seven months, everything was going to plan and, except for a six-week lay-off when my back gave up on me, I was all set to reach my target. Then the Covid-19 pandemic hit, early in 2020, and the golf course became out of bounds for two entire months. So, I adjusted the plan. My new commitment became to hit at least fifty 40 or 50-yard pitches every day (in the orchard at the side of our garden).

The honest truth is that, without the defined goal on my vision board, those two side-lining, unavoidable circumstances would have probably stopped me playing or practicing until it had all passed. But because I had a target and a process to follow, I was never going to let myself down. And, as a result, three things happened:

1. I learned to enjoy my daily trips out to the orchard to hit golf balls into the distance
2. When lockdown lifted, and I got back on the course, everyone knew I had improved
3. I failed to hit my target. Yes, that is right I did not reduce my handicap to 15

As of August 2020, my official handicap was 16.3. But here is the thing. By the time you read this book, I will be playing off a handicap below 15 (because I have set a new SMART target). If I hadn't set the original goal, the events of 2020 would probably have stopped me progressing, and I would still be at 20 or worse (and not enjoying my golf nearly as much as I am). But ultimately, I am now a better golfer.

LESSON FIVE

It is lonely out there: walls, coaches and friends

I have talked at length about how the wall at Campden Hill Lawn Tennis Club represents patience, persistence and process. In the preceding chapters, I introduced the idea of having a specific goal or target to aim for. Now, I want to look at the importance of strength, support, reliability, guidance and coaching as you develop into the person you want to be – the person who will make you the happiest. By definition, a wall is a pretty solid thing and hitting one in a vehicle, with your fists, or by running into it is going to cause some damage. But, as we have seen, it can also represent something that can rebound ideas, return your efforts so that you can have another shot, send you new challenges and stretch your potential. Walls can also be an indicator that danger lies ahead, set out boundaries that should not be crossed, and protect people, property and ideas. And finally, a wall can be a support when you are weary, something to lean on or a platform you can climb on to get a better view of the landscape. Walls are many things and can represent a range of analogies and anecdotes in a business environment. But in all these scenarios, the defining feature of a wall is that it is steadfast and reliable. Unfortunately, people are not.

I have worked with and alongside dozens of people throughout my career. Some were colleagues, teammates, and collaborators; while others were mentors, managers or those I nurtured in their positions. There have been role models I admired and studied from a distance, and those closer to home who gave me guidance, tough love and the generosity of their time. I've formed strong relationships with most, found others a pain in the neck, and some have even become my very best friends. But here is the thing about people. None of us is perfect, and we will all let each other down from time to time.

In chapter five of this book, I'll talk about how my dad influenced me to look down throughout my life while Peter Henesey Smith encouraged me to look up. Yet, my dad was a great dad in most other ways. In chapter four, I mention people who stood alongside my early endeavours, before turning and playing their part in bringing them down. And you'll also hear how a random conversation with a former rival got me back on my feet. In the next two chapters, I will reveal how I was very much the person to blame for causing other people's pain. We are all human and are fallible as a result. My point here is that a wall is not made of a single brick. It is a support network that draws strength from the other bricks around it and stands together to form something immovable. If you look back on your life, I do not doubt that you will see the same. A closely woven fabric of influencers, for better or worse, who shaped the person you have become today.

Today I choose my wall

As I said, there are no perfect people in the world; but there are good people who will do their best to support you, advise you and, likewise, return your influence on them with interest. In our early lives, we all get the wall that we are born with. It starts with a parent or two; then siblings and wider family are introduced, along with friends and eventually school. There comes the point in your life, however, when the wall you are born with becomes the one you deserve. You cannot escape your family, but you can decide who else joins the party.

The best thing about the network of influencers and influences you surround yourself with today is that you get to choose every single member of the team. Realising this was a revelation for me and is why Mastermind Groups have become an integral part of my business life for the past ten years. Life and running a business, in particular, is too complicated and unpredictable to be able to manage it successfully on your own. And the great thing about building a strong wall is that the combined support between every brick covers the well-intentioned mistakes and failings we are all prone to from time to time. When the toughest of life's catastrophes collide with a strong and resilient love-bound wall, there is no way the circumstance is going to bring it down.

As a little exercise, why not draw, list or visualise the wall around you today. Ask yourself which bricks (people and influences) support and strengthen your goals and which are the weak spots. I'm not suggesting you totally disown your oldest friend because they are the very epitome of pessimism; or that you cut Uncle Pete from your Christmas card list because he is the worst gossip ever. But you might want to rearrange the pieces.

Maybe you could shuffle the time and distance between people, bringing the valuable influences nearer and pushing a few doors closed for a while if necessary. It may even be that you spot some gaping holes that need filling in your wall and one of your goals becomes to find a coach, a mentor or someone you can trust to take on the burden of admin that is weighing you down for three hours each day.

LESSON SIX

Unforced errors and taking responsibility

This book has been planned for a while, and the version you're reading is actually my third attempt at completing the task. Part of the reason was that I no longer enjoy, play or take much of an interest in tennis. Yet, every time I sat down to write a few pages, take advice about the structure or stand on a stage to talk about business, I could not escape my history. Much of what I know, teach, and who I am today is because of my background as a tennis coach. Eventually, I gave in to the inescapable truth and decided to tell my story. The current reality of that story, however, is that I have fallen in love with another sport, and it too is full of powerful and pertinent analogies, anecdotes and business lessons.

I mentioned it briefly a few lessons back. But in the final part of this chapter, I want to explain why the lessons learned from golf are fundamentally even better for your business than the valuable lessons learned from tennis.

If you have watched tennis on TV, you will be familiar with the term 'unforced error', where a player makes a mistake rather than being outplayed or beaten by a better shot. But you will also hear the commentators of a tennis match make comments like 'too good' or 'that was simply unplayable' as they add their expert analysis to what you are watching with your own two eyes. You do not hear that in golf commentary. When you are playing golf, every single error you make is unforced in the sense that only you are responsible. And in business, the single biggest mistake a business owner can make is to look around for someone to blame when the ball is played down the line and out of their floundering reach. The main reason for this is that in business, as when playing golf, the only competition is yourself. It is why the handicap system works so well on a golf course – creating a level playing field where everyone can compete on the same course regardless of skill, experience or the quality of their clubs.

Let's say that four players make up a foursome one sunny afternoon on the local course and are playing off handicaps of 12, 15, 17 and 18 respectively. In effect, while they can still have a bit of friendly competition among themselves to decide who buys the drinks at the nineteenth hole, each player is really just challenging themselves. The performance of their colleagues can (and often does) affect how they play emotionally, but it has zero physical impact. One player having the round of their life does not impede or open opportunities for another. Each player's score is independent of anyone else in their group or anywhere on the course.

What can you do to reduce your handicap?

In business, the rules of the game are exactly the same. All businesses (even the ones playing the same game) vary in subtle or significant ways, have different ideal customers, are driven by unique passions and aim for their own goals and targets. No one business can blame another for its failure or success. I do not know of any business, in any sector, where there are not enough customers to go around. (I have to put a caveat in here because some businesses do launch without first identifying a need for what they are selling. But if you have competition that is succeeding at what you do, you should be able to, as well). And, the worst excuse a business owner can give me for their failing business is that they don't have enough time – because everyone has the same amount of time and the world's super-successful people seem to manage. If one company in a sector suffers from Government legislation, global pandemics, or other external influences, every other one will too. And the challenges of staff, cash flow, suppliers, marketing and getting products out on time are the same for every business on the planet. If you want to be successful in business, the one thing you need to get your head around more than anything else is that you are responsible for everything.

If you are going to blame the competition, the economy or the people who make the rules – you should not be in business. It is as simple as that. But here is the good news. As well as getting out on the golf course to test your abilities against other players in the real world, you can book time on the driving range, the putting greens or a whole industry selling home or office based practice equipment. (I would not recommend hitting a golf ball against a wall, however, as the ricochet would be unpredictable, and you'd probably lose a lot of balls. But the principle is the same).

My point is, of course, that there are no unforced errors in business. As a business owner, you are responsible for everything that goes wrong and everything that goes well. You can build your team around you: a solid, reliable wall that can help take the weight, bounce ideas back to you and give you a firm foundation to build on. You can find coaches who will help to develop your skills, teach you new ones and fine tune your handicap so you can compete at higher levels in line with your goals. And you can deal with anything that comes your way because you know you have the strength of a strong business all around you - a business you built, one brick at a time.

2

SEEMA

Turning tragedy and guilt into focus and hope

Sometimes life throws things in your path that are just too big and too catastrophic to handle. And the harshest of life's lessons is surely death. But when it is the unexpected, untimely, unjust death of a younger sister, there are no words deep enough to express how it makes you feel. I cannot even call it pain because it does not come close. Loss is nothing more than a word in those circumstances, and guilt is a raging bear that tears at your heart and darkens the far reaches of your mind. Your life certainly changes when things like that become a part of its tapestry.

It was a Wednesday morning, 15th August 2001, and it was scorching hot. I was at the tennis club getting ready for another busy day in the middle of my sixty-hour-per-week, go-go-go, no time for stopping lifestyle. My recurring back pain was creeping up again, the temperature was stifling, and weeks of stress-charged sleepless nights were taking their toll.

The phone rang, and it was my dad. I was irritable (not surprising considering the circumstances of my life at that moment) and made no effort to hide my impatience at his intrusion. "What do you want?"

He ignored my tone, as only a love-blinded parent could, and replied, "Your sister isn't at the airport".

"So what? You know what they're like, they'll be on the next flight – I've got to go, I've got work to do..." I hung up, picked the shirt that would best show off my toned torso to my students' mums and finished breakfast on the go as I made my way out to the tennis courts. There was a niggle in the back of my mind all morning. But the heat, my list of things to do, and the addictive rush of the under-pressure go-getter existence buried it deeper and deeper as the day went on. When dad rang back a couple of hours later, however, that thought came rushing to the surface once more.

"It's Dad, can you come to the house so we can work out what to do?"

Perhaps it was the blatant attempt to ignore my intuition that forced my reaction – I don't know – whatever the reason I instantly reached for my irritated defence again.

"Bloody hell Dad, I'm busy teaching. Why is this important?"

"Just come, Ash," he replied.

You know the cold all over, sick to your stomach hollowness that descends when you first hear bad news? Well, I hadn't been told any specific detail at that moment, but I'm sure my face must have shown I knew something terrible had happened. I barked a few orders to my team then got in the car to drive to my parents' home.

I was greeted at the door by two police officers, helmets in hand, and hardly daring to meet my gaze. They began to tell me how Seema, my precious baby sister, had died in a car crash in South Africa. But I already knew. Even as the emptiness taunting me during that short drive was replaced by a bloody dizziness, almost bringing me to my knees, I knew. I didn't need to listen to them. I didn't *want* to listen to them. I simply wanted to curl up into a ball and die alongside a friend I would never see again.

Before I go on, please don't think there will be any of those 'everything happens for a reason' platitudes presented within this story. Losing my sister, like the untimely death of any young person is nothing but an unavoidable tragedy – there is no reason, no 'greater good'. Any personal strength, clarity of purpose or determination to make my life count is not and never could be a fair exchange for her life.

But here is the point. What happened to Seema happened. I cannot do anything about it or reverse it. And the reality is – guilt, regret, and sadness only have limited value for those that have to live with it. The other inescapable truth for those who have to live with loss is – you still have to live. So all I can do to honour her memory is live the best life I can. That's what I hope you get from my book; and this chapter in particular.

Seema Taylor and her best friend Fiona Marks worked in school in Cairo, Egypt. It is easy to say nice things about people you love at their funeral, but these two veritable forces of nature genuinely *were* special. They lived for adventure and travel, for the moment; and for making a difference.

Even at the interview, when they went for the same job (there was only one job on offer), they both finished their interview by telling Gerard, the Head Teacher, they would only take the position if the other one were employed too. Such was their impact on Gerard he created an extra role to facilitate the pair. We didn't know that. We learned about this, and many other exploits, experiences and influences they left in the school's memory when Gerard flew over for their funeral. They were both 27 years old when they died and packed so much into their short but abundant time on this planet.

At the time, all I knew about Seema's life was that she lived and worked in a school in Egypt and that she did crazy things during her holidays. I probably thought, somewhere in the back of my mind, that she should settle down and take a bit more responsibility before it is too late. I even planned to serve her with a big-brother chat about growing up and building a future, when I got around to it. Even as I write those words, the feelings of guilt and regret are bubbling. But I have learned how to deal with them. And while the sadness is still there, I know what happened to them is not my fault. There is a huge lesson to learn there, and I will come back to that later in this chapter.

Some of my sister's adventuring exploits included travelling to India to visit family I've never even met. She went skydiving in New Zealand, backpacking around Australia and helped build a school in Nepal. But on this occasion, their last adventure as it turned out, Seema and Fiona had booked a month off to go to South Africa. When we had their photos developed, they showed it had been an amazing trip, full of off-the-beaten-track explorations. But, while they were driving to the airport, heading for a stop-off in the UK before going back to Egypt, an articulated lorry hit them. Witnesses said the driver was on the phone and clearly hadn't seen the traffic slowing abruptly in front of him. We later learned the traffic jam had been caused by a tow truck driver lighting a fire to cause a distraction and an accident deliberately. He figured he might pick up some extra work that day so he could feed his family. Neither men were charged for their part in the girls' tragic death.

A year after they died, the school invited us to Egypt, along with Fiona's family. What greeted us was a celebration of their lives at the opening of a new wing of the school named in their honour. It brought home the fact that my life and the life of my little sister couldn't have gone in more opposite directions. I had visions of creating a business empire, and she loved the simple joys of exploring, discovering, living and learning in the company of real people in exotic lands. My life was driven by the shallow pursuit of future riches and hers by the depth of value she could find in the present day.

I will say again – nothing could be worth the price of Seema's life. But my consolation is she taught me how to live a better one in the time I have. Please believe me when I say that, because it is not a flippant statement, and neither was it a realisation I arrived at easily. First, I had to battle through the avalanche of anger, guilt and regret that engulfed me.

At first, I took cover behind my natural management mode. I arranged the funeral and reception, handled the paperwork and repatriation of the bodies, communicated with their employers, friends and family, and was the shoulder for everyone else to cry on. After my first reaction in front of those police officers at my parents' front door, I don't think anyone saw me openly cry until I collapsed on a psychiatrist's couch several years later. The guilt that burned inside me came from two places. How I'd responded to my dad's phone call while wrapped up inside my own ambition (although he never mentioned it again). And the fact Seema had lived an extraordinary life, and I knew very little about it. Oh, what I wouldn't give to go back in time and hear of her journeys, encounters and the life lessons she could teach me.

Guilt is a natural reaction, one that every innocent person has when tragedy strikes close to home. It stems from the questions we pose ourselves that begin with 'what if?' – then we traipse through all the things we could have done differently and the times we should have paid more attention or shown how much we care. But the reality is, if we could live those moments again, we wouldn't have acted any different – because hindsight is not really a wonderful thing. Present-sight is far more precious. And that, in essence, is the point of sharing this story with you. Today is the most important day of your life – consider what you do with it and don't waste any opportunity.

I will never see Seema again. Hear her voice or listen to her 'laugh till she cried'. She won't be there to stand up for me, like so many times before, even when I am wrong. I will never have the chance to be an uncle to her children or her an aunt to mine. That's gone forever. Nor will I get to interrogate another of her wayward boyfriends. And I will never get to see what she did next or if she would have gone on to change the world. In less selfish moments, however, I like to think that somewhere in the world young adults are recalling the impact Seema Taylor had on their lives.

And I hope that, because of Seema's legacy, everyone who reads this book is reminded to live life in the present. Yes, plan for your future, but not at the expense of today. I hope as you soak up this and other stories from my life that you have many years ahead of you, but I urge you not to take the ones you are living now for granted. Seema and Fiona had so much they wanted to do, and they lived like they didn't have a moment to lose or spend waiting for it to happen. Their 27 years were filled with more stories, adventures and achievements than most people fit into a long lifetime. And the more I contacted the people they worked with, taught and encountered as they travelled, the more I learned the depth of the impression they left behind. It was a short life, but it was a life worth living, and they lived it to the full.

In the six short lessons that follow, I want you to keep my sister and her best friend's story in your mind. And make these three rules the foundation of the lessons I'm going to share next:

1. Today is the only day you get to 'do' anything. Tomorrow will only ever be a plan.
2. The only value to come from regret (whether guilty or innocent) is to learn the lesson, toughen-up and do better.
3. Ask yourself regularly what matters most in your life and apply yourself to those goals daily.

LESSON ONE

Recognise the value of your time

Do you know the most common phone call received by domestic alarm fitting companies each day? That's right; it is to request the installation of a better security system. But – it's usually *the day after* their house has been burgled. That's when they finally take action. The call is probably something the owner has thought about for years. And while the insurance may adequately cover the material loss, that dirty feeling of someone rummaging through your personal belongings and walking unchallenged around your home goes deep. So you finally take action, albeit a day too late.

It is an old saying, but profoundly true nonetheless, that tomorrow never comes. I guarantee this is not the first time the idea of taking action today has been presented to you. I could reel off dozens of 'carpe diem' style clichés, throw YOLO at you or tell you that 'It's not the number of breaths we take, but the number of moments that take our breath away'. These messages are over-hyped and overused – but it doesn't lessen the truth of the matter. Our days are numbered, and most of them are wasted on unworthy pursuits. The only reason people don't act is because they believe there will always be a tomorrow and tragedy only ever happens to people on the news or in the movies. We take life for granted because we've been waking up day after day for decades and we expect to for decades to come. Most people live life in a repetitive rut.

Don't get me wrong here. I'm not talking about the chances of today being your last. What I really want you to consider is the value of today, even if you live to be one hundred twenty years old.

£1,500 per day

Imagine you wake up tomorrow morning and there on your side-table, tightly wrapped in bands of coloured paper, are three piles of twenty-pound notes. After the obligatory double-take and quick scan of the room for hidden cameras or pranksters, you notice a note pinned to one of the stacks. It says, simply 'you have 24-hours in which to spend this money and every pound that remains at the end of the day will be lost to you forever'.

You lie back on your pillow for a moment, wondering how you would spend the money (if this were not the dream that it clearly must be). But as you contemplate this thought and wait to wake up, it dawns on you that you *are* awake and so you reach for one of the bundles and start to count. One, two, three... There are twenty-five, crisp, clean twenty-pound notes in each of the three piles, giving you a total of £1,500. Picking up the instructions once more, you notice the text has mysteriously changed. It now spells out two rules: you cannot add to or invest the money, and you cannot give any of it away. Then, as you read the final word, the paper disintegrates into a glitter-tinted puff of smoke, right in front of your eyes. And it becomes clear to you there is an unusual kind of magic in the air today.

What would you spend your £1,500 on, if you only had a day to spend it? Here are a few of the answers people call out when I've presented this story from the stage:

- Gucci or Christian Louboutin shoes
- Virtual Reality theatre system
- Focal or B&O headphones
- MacBook Pro
- Full body massage chair
- OLED Flatscreen TV
- Portable 4k drone
- A treadmill workstation
- MALOUF Italian bed sheets
- Indoor sauna or hot tub
- Louis Vuitton or Prada handbag

I'm sure you will have similar things go through your head when you imagine the scenario. What I notice about the list above is that, although maybe a little lavish and designer-orientated, most of the items are at least practical. A valid and sensible argument could be presented to justify the purchase of each one (maybe not the treadmill workstation).

At the end of your day of spending, as the adrenaline-fuelled rush of purchasing beyond your usual budget dies down and buyer's remorse is pushed aside because it wasn't your money in the first place, you descend into a satisfied snooze. And just as you drop off, you see the £220 you had left over vanish in the twinkling of an eye. You dream of superyachts, living on a private island in the Caribbean and awake to the expectation of champagne and lobster sandwiches for breakfast. Then, as reality dawns and you glance at the new Tag Heuer digital alarm clock on your side-table, you see another three stacks of money and a note that reads, 'same rules apply'. Once again, the paper vaporises as soon as it has delivered its message and the magic begins all over again.

Day after day, the same thing happens. And, by the middle of the second week, your spending choices are getting more frivolous and, quite frankly, ridiculous. I mean, I know a purple-flamed, two-headed electric guitar hanging on the wall looks cool, but do you even know how to play it?

Work through the whole scenario for yourself, and be honest. I think you'll agree that as each £1,500 a day passed, and you increasingly took your spending power for granted, you'd begin to forget the value it represented. You may have guessed by now where I am going with this and if I was to change the number to something more specific – let's say £1,440 – it might confirm your suspicions. But just in case the message behind my anecdote hasn't landed yet, let me explain.

Do you know you have 1,440 minutes available to spend each and every day of your life? It is impossible to get any more, you can't pass them on to anyone else, and not a single minute can be saved up for a rainy day. Each minute is only available to be spent within the 24 hours after they are delivered each morning. The reality is, of course, that a few hundred will be used up before you even wake up, but if you know anything about the science of sleep – those are minutes well-spent.

Treating time like money is such a powerful concept, albeit not a new one. The English language has long been full of terminology like, 'How have you been spending your time?' and 'I recommend Bobby invests a bit more time revising for his exams'. But I want you to start deliberately thinking in this way: even if just to stop you taking time for granted. If you wanted to really put this hypothesis to the test, you could even try this little strategy.

I challenge you to go to the bank and withdraw £480 in twenty-pound notes to represent the 480 minutes in an eight-hour working day. Then, whenever you let someone *interrupt you; or a meeting you have agreed to attend turns out to be a complete waste of time, or you become distracted by other tasks that are beneath your pay grade – you have to tear up the appropriate number of twenty-minute notes. (You might be better to give the money to an appropriate charity – but actually losing it from your pocket will do you good.) It is not inconceivable that many people reading this book will value their working time in the region of £500 per day; so this test will be an apt one. And I promise you that physically giving the money away works.

**Scientific studies have shown that when a person in the full flow of concentrated effort is interrupted, it can take up to twenty minutes for their brain to return to the same level of efficient and productive momentum.*

Before leaving this chapter about recognising the value of your time, I want to make a few personal observations about time well spent. And, while I teach the principle described above as the same for everyone, I understand that you might consider some of the following as my opinion, so feel free to take them or leave them.

- Lifestyle is a wonderful thing: you don't have to be a millionaire to be considered happy, successful or having made it in life – a lifestyle business only needs to support the lifestyle you want
- Not all distractions are a waste of time: for some people, planned time out is the best way to maximise the effectiveness of the time they put into whatever goal they are pursuing
- Sleep and rest are time well spent: there is a clear line between laziness and getting enough rest – it differs from person to person, but once you've worked out your optimum work/rest ratio use it well
- Not all hours are equal: as with understanding the level of rest you require to get the most out of your waking hours, you should experiment with working at different times of the day to learn when is your best time
- Outsource your time: while my example said you can't borrow, lend or carry time over, I have found that outsourcing administrative tasks in my work and life frees up time for me to spend elsewhere

I'll cover a few of these points in more detail later in the book, but for now – happy spending.

LESSON TWO

Accept that life is not fair

It was 25th May 2003, the end of a season where QPR finished fourth in the Second Division, just three points shy of automatic promotion. We had beaten Oldham in the play-off semi-final and begrudgingly travelled to play Cardiff on their turf – the Millennium Stadium. How could that be chosen as a neutral ground for the final? Well, Wembley was in redevelopment and, as the stand-in national stadium, the battleground had been staged across the border.

For non-football fans, you have to understand that nothing is more painful for a club of QPR's history and stature than living in the third tier of English football. It is one of those things that just isn't right, especially in the wake of our near neighbours, Chelsea, purchasing their way into European status in the last twenty years.

Having finished two places above Cardiff in the league and harbouring every expectation that we would end the day one division nearer our rightful place the following season; we started singing. After edging the first half, Ian Holloway's team talk must have been inspiring, because we looked like winners for the whole of the second. But the one goal we needed didn't come. No goals on 90-minutes meant extra-time, and the stalemate continued until six minutes from time. Then, totally against the run-of-play, our most stalwart of defensive reliabilities, Danny Shittu, slipped and we were one-down. If you've thought ahead while reading this short summary of an uneventful football match and expect it to end in heroic response – think again. That, in a nutshell, was that. We lost a game that we should have won hands down. And I unequivocally and without a hint of bias believe we would have won that match nineteen times out of twenty if it were played again – especially if it was at a genuinely neutral ground (not that I am bitter).

So, here is my point. Life is not like a computer game where you can just start again. You cannot save your place when you are 90% of the way through a challenging level (in case you lose your last life in the final battle). What is done is done, and you cannot reverse the hand life has dealt you, whether it is through your fault, someone else's or just plain bad luck. And you have only two choices. You can live with guilt and regret; your head and heart weighed down by the past and questioning the injustice of it all. Or, you can learn the lessons, pay respects, be grateful for the good things you still have in your life, and move on. You have two choices, yes, but in truth, there is no choice at all. You either make the most of your life, or you don't.

QPR had better days to come, and the following year we won the league, avoiding the lottery of the play-offs and re-established ourselves in the Championship. Look out Premiership – a sleeping giant is waiting to return.

What is it in your life or business that is holding you back? If it is a seemingly insurmountable wall in front of you, read on, because I will deal with that shortly. But, for many people reading this book, it will be a disappointment in things that happened yesterday, last year or even ten years ago. Every ounce of logic tells you to let it go and live the life that you have today, but too often intense feelings of injustice, bitterness and regret seem to weld us to the past. I know how you feel – I've fought that wall on many occasions – but I urge you to cut your losses, let go of your attachment to yesterday, and move on. It is the only choice worth making.

LESSON THREE

The marathon runner

I'm not a marathon runner, nor have I ever really enjoyed running for sport or fitness. But as a spectator, and a universal sports fan, I can't help but admire endurance athletes of all types. Just that willingness to continue when every fibre of your body cries out 'stop' and their ability to concentrate on a monotonous step-at-a-time process to reach a gigantic distant goal. What triathletes, ironmen and ironwomen, road race cyclists, marathon runners and other long-haul competitors achieve is truly remarkable. And alongside the example set by their superhuman hearts and minds, there is a lot we can learn from their method.

The title of this book, Hitting the Wall, alludes to the obsessive hitting of a tennis ball against a wall and other analogies I will refer to later. But perhaps the most famous use of the phrase is its reference to that point in a marathon runner's endeavour where all the training goes to pot and willpower is their last defence. As I said, I have not faced that sensation specifically, but I can positively identify with the concept – and I suspect you can too.

To get a better understanding of the experience and see what lessons we can garner from it, I interviewed my neighbour, Chris, who has completed over fifty marathons, and nine ultra-marathons. He explained to me that he has 'hit the wall' twice. Once during a fifty-five-mile ultra-marathon in South Africa and previous to that during a half marathon in Barbados. Yes, with the list of achievements described above, it is surprising that nine miles into a meagre thirteen and bit mile stroll he would have to face such an ordeal. But there is a lesson in that too: take nothing for granted. Here is what Chris said when I asked him to describe his experience:

The race was starting at 7 am, from Barbados Airport, and we arrived in a bit of a hurry expecting to be able to find food or water to fuel up for the race. But Grantley Adams Airport, Bridgetown, is not Heathrow and nothing was open. Add to that our rushed arrival, the early hour, the devastating heat and a dozen other slight interferences which on their own wouldn't usually have made any difference. The race started, and I quickly got into the rhythm and pace I had planned for this event – for seven or eight miles, everything was fine.

But the eighth mile felt a bit odd. Then, as I passed the next mile marker, it was like running into a six-foot wall of reinforced glass. I just felt empty. An overpowering hopelessness descended through my body, sucking the energy from more than my legs, arms and heart. The dull ache of starvation raged through my brain as vividly as the thirst from my throat, and all internal communication went diabolic. Providing you've achieved a certain level of fitness; distance running is as much about controlling the mind as it is your body – so when attacked from both angles, you have no chance. At that moment, I found myself subject to an all-out physical and emotional assault, and if I'd had any energy at all, it would have exploded into a rage at the injustice of it all. I was confused, momentarily estranged from any control over my body and slumped in a heap, unable to comprehend how a seasoned runner like me could have got it so wrong.

Listening to Chris's story, it reminds me that sometimes life just happens and there is no explanation. Other times we may have taken our eye off the ball, the situation for granted or made one too many assumptions. We can react in lots of ways, and sometimes we surprise ourselves. But the important thing is that you pick yourself up, fight another day and determine to go on and achieve far more significant and spectacular wins. What Chris and other ultra-athletes like him do is amazing. I can't say I am envious, because running is not my thing. But there is so much about winning in life you could take from the mind-over-emotion determination and one-foot-after-another experiences of people like Chris.

LESSON FOUR

Self-pity is self-sabotage

I felt guilt and regret at what happened to Seema because that is what happens. It is a glitch in human nature that we tend to blame ourselves when something clearly isn't our fault, even if it is only the language we use that reveals this trait. It is why we say, "I'm sorry for your loss" when we hear that a friend's father has died, or "I'm sorry to hear that" when someone has been made redundant. Hearing bad news doesn't make it your fault – you are not responsible – and yet, for a moment at least, you feel the weight.

When the loss is personal, of course, the feelings and emotions are intensified, and that is what makes them so potentially damaging. In the cold light of day, when the rational mind has hold of your reins, or if you are on the outside talking to someone else, it is so obvious that it is not your fault. But at that moment, as the weight of the situation comes crashing down, and sometimes even two decades later, you become determined to blame yourself. And in extreme circumstances, you will even go trawling through scenarios where you could have done better, acted differently or simply paid more attention. You then find yourself inventing reasons to point the finger at yourself.

I can tell you two things from my experience. Neither will bring Seema back, but they could change your life and the lives of those closest to you forever.

Firstly, being angry will not help you deal with the past. The perfectly reasonable anger I felt towards the two men whose actions led to Seema and Fiona's deaths cannot help the girls and didn't benefit me. All my anger did was make getting on with life more painful and a harder struggle. And not only for me. My anger created unhappiness in other people's lives too. The second big lesson is that living in the past sabotages the future. I'm not suggesting you cannot look back, reminisce on precious memories or even shed a tear from time to time – but living there will ruin the life you are fortunate enough to have in front of you.

Self-pity is self-sabotage, and it is deeply selfish. You have got to find a way to move on. And that starts with having honest conversations with yourself and with the people around you—the ones affected by the same issue. The key word in that last sentence is 'honest'. As I mentioned earlier in the book, my initial defence was to hide behind the administrative processes and trying to be the strong one for everyone else. But that was nothing but a front, which is why it ultimately failed. Because not only was I kidding myself, everyone else could see through my weak disguise.

Some of the walls we face in life need to be broken down. Others, like the one I hit ten thousand tennis balls against in my youth, are there to teach us, challenge us and shape us into better performers. Walls that represent heartbreak and loss cannot be broken because they cannot be changed – but they can become strong foundations from which we can start again or build better lives.

Someone once asked me if I thought people who have been through great tragedies became stronger and more aware; therefore hold an advantage over those whose lives have been sugar-coated. And, although I certainly wouldn't recommend it as a strategy to pursue, I think yes, that is probably true.

LESSON FIVE

Ask yourself the big questions

I want you to think about two things in this chapter. What do you want from life, and what is your time worth to you? Hopefully, you have already bought into the idea of spending minutes like currency and visualising how most people are guilty of recklessly throwing their time around without a thought for its value. Now, I'd like to bring together the idea of spending your time directly on the things that are most valuable to you in life. Those dreams, activities and objectives that give you the most happiness and enjoyment.

If you are a business owner, for example, I assume you decided to pursue that career path for lifestyle, financial or altruistic reasons. Whatever your motivation, I am sure the first business plan you presented to your family or your investors didn't have the line: I plan to work long stressful hours and lose sleep worrying about cash, deadlines or lack of sales. And yet, we are all familiar with the statistics around business closures in the first year and many more struggling to make a profit. Behind every business that fails, and for the ones still just about hanging on today, there is a story of poor time management, lack of financial planning, and head-in-the-sand unfounded optimism. So, what do you want to achieve from your business? And how do you want your business to influence your life positively?

When I started my first business, and particularly as I began mixing with other entrepreneurs at networking or training events, I was introduced to the term lifestyle-business. It sounded almost romantic to me and something to aim for. Yet it seemed that the bigger business owners and the go-getters would sneer at the concept. It was as if the idea was an excuse for not 'giving it your all' or settling for being one of the crowd. Maybe, unconsciously, I was influenced by these big thinkers into missing the point – and perhaps that is why I ended up blowing my time-budget trying to become the millionaire they said I should be. I'll come back to my business story later in the book. But, for now, let me explain my definition of a lifestyle business, and why I now think it should be every business owner's aspiration.

Building a business that supports your lifestyle

The quote "Nobody on their deathbed has ever said 'I wish I had spent more time at the office'" hits the nail squarely on the head. Life is short, and the reality is that none of us knows how much time we have left. That makes time the most valuable asset available to any person on the planet. So, your business goals should start with your life goals. Ask yourself what is important to you. If it is spending time with your family, don't confuse that with earning enough to put your children through university. Maybe you want to travel and see the world before you die so you set about working yourself into an early grave before you get a chance to book some flights. Or you could be on a mission to create financial security for you and your family and after another night sleeping on the office floor find they've left you to find love elsewhere. It could just be that you want to enjoy walks in the woods, weekends with your partner and four holidays a year with your children, not even caring where you can afford to go. Well, what is stopping you?

Decide what you want your life to be and plan to start living that life right now. Yes, you may have to make some sacrifices, but make sure they are short-term. There is no silver bullet or shortcut to success, and hard work is a given: but sixty or seventy-hours-a-week is no life to live. Believe me – I have tried both lifestyles, and I can tell you one is a thankless route to an early grave and the other is one hundred per cent possible.

All you need to do is clarify what you want your life to be today and plan to start living that way. The caveat is, of course, that your ambitions should be reasonable (in line with what I described above), but they can also be ambitious. I promise you – mine are.

Here are the fundamentals you need to employ to create your own lifestyle-fulfilling business:

- Describe your perfect lifestyle: today, in one-year and in five years' time
- Spend deliberate time every day working on high-value activities that move you towards your goals
- Outsource low-value activities that waste your goal-directed time, cause you stress or cloud your vision

- Devise strategies to increase income, reduce workload, free-up your time and ease your mind
- Take responsibility for everything that happens in your life/business: whether it is your fault or not
- Get a deep understanding of your business numbers: make them work for you and your lifestyle
- When working 'in' the business make sure it's because *only you* can do those things
- Treat your time like a bank account: 1,440 valuable minutes per day

This strategy is not a pipedream or a fantasy. I believe every small business owner can and should be planning their work and living life in this way. And I'll be unpacking some of these things in more detail later in the book.

LESSON SIX

Legacy

I am going to finish this chapter as a tribute to my sister and her best friend, Fiona. But also, as a summary of the key things I want you to take from what we have discussed so far.

Encouraging you to seize the day is a well-worn cliché, I know. But Seema's story, alongside the proven, practical and one hundred per cent doable strategies I've shared could, quite literally, change your life – from today onwards. But only if you decide you are going to take action. The irony of that statement is that I don't want you just to get busy doing any old stuff. I want you to put time aside to think deeply and seriously about what is important to you and what you want your life to be. You could go even further and ask what your life should mean.

Have you ever been to a funeral and smiled as you listened to friends and family say lovely things about their dearly departed? I often wonder at the impact on that life if those things were said while they were able to respond. We are a funny species really. Every other animal on the planet spends its days or nights seeking food, taking shelter, fighting for survival and passing on its genes. We, however, wonder at the meaning of our lives; dream of what tomorrow might bring, plan for our futures, create magnificent machines and tantalising technology, let emotions rule our actions and care what others think about us.

Let's imagine you live to be one hundred and twenty years old, with all your faculties intact and still able to complete nine holes on your local golf course. You may laugh – but if you are under sixty today, the medical advances in science might just make you get there! Either way, humour me for a moment. So, you live a long and healthy life, and the end comes suddenly, but peacefully, as a result of a little too much wine and a mix up with your blue pills one evening.

What would you like people to say as they gather at your wake and reflect on how you influenced their lives? And I know it will matter to you because if you have reached this far in the book, I know you are someone who cares. We are social animals who gain comfort from belonging, achieve incredible things when working in groups, and are influenced by each other's examples, stories and leadership. So, what you do this day and for the rest of your days matters. Not only in *your* life, but in the lives of everyone whose journey intersects yours.

But that is not even the biggest lesson I want you to take from this chapter of my book.

Before Seema died, I lived my life head down, busy-busy-busy, frantically trying to make as much money as possible so I could hoard it for the future. The news those two police officers delivered on my parents' doorstep drove me headlong into the cruellest of irreversible walls. But after the initial shock (and of all the things I've told you so far this is the thing I am least proud of) I still chose to bury my hurt, disregard the warning, and carry on in exactly the same way regardless. And it was not until another wall challenged me (one I'll tell you about in the next chapter) that the lessons of Seema's life hit home. So, while you are reading this, please avoid my mistake. Don't wait for tragedy to strike before you wake up. Act today.

My sister's life taught me lots of things, but the biggest is that you can live a life of happiness today. You do not need to chase distant horizons; you can choose to enjoy the things that you have right in front of you at this moment in time. Yes, Seema and Fiona worked hard, dreamed big, and planned exciting adventures for the future, but never at the cost of their present. Their lives were not about what tomorrow might bring or building a retirement fund that might never happen. They spent their time 'at the time' and loved every moment. They lived richly.

I hope to have many years ahead of me, but I know this for sure. Whenever the time comes for me to look up at the lid of my coffin, it will be with a smile and no regrets. There will be no 'I wish I had...' in my heart, and everyone I know will know that Ash Taylor cared.

3

DADDY LOOK AT ME

Does the business support my life or rule it?

The story I am about to tell you is not one I am proud of. In many ways, it is not even my story at all. It is Jace's story, and I could not be prouder of the person Jace was then and has grown into today. If you are a parent and a business owner, I have no doubt you will have a similar story somewhere in your past or perhaps yet to come. And whether you are a parent or not, I urge you not to ignore this wall: either when it hits you (as it inevitably will one day) or as I share my version of it now. You see, some of the walls I describe in this book hit me harder, others taught me a wider variety of lessons; but this one was undeniably the most important. This one gets to the core of what really matters and why any of us does what we do. Because it is one thing knowing (or kidding yourself that you know) why you get up every morning and go to work; but it is completely different to act in line with that clear perspective.

It was 24th October 2011, and the afternoon of Jace's eighth birthday. After a busy day, I had just about managed to pick Jace up from her mum's on time, and now we were off to spend some 'just us' birthday time in the park. It was part-one of what had been planned as a wonderful birthday afternoon and evening together. I can't remember the conversation in the car on the way to the park, except that it was pretty one-sided because my mind was on something big happening back at the office. It wasn't that I begrudged taking that time away from work, in fact, I had been looking forward to it for days (I was not that bad a dad), but it was fair to say I hadn't fully 'arrived at the scene' just yet. An entrepreneur's life *should* be challenging, exciting and unpredictable, shouldn't it? Surely that is what we all signed up for? At least, that's what I thought in those days.

I distinctly remember the sun shining in my eyes through the trees as we arrived at the park, and as I locked the car door, my phone rang. It was the important call I had been expecting for the last hour, and I answered it within two rings, as usual. My mind was instantly engulfed in the issue being described at the other end of the line as I walked and talked, hand and phone-to-ear; the other hand holding that of the little voice walking and talking beside me. Then my other phone rang. Yes, like every responsible business owner, I had two phones so I could maintain my work-life balance and keep both sides of my life in their respective places. But like every irresponsible business owner, with good intentions at heart, they were both kept on at all times just in case someone needed to get hold of me – and, of course, my best customers had both numbers so they could always reach me.

With both hands occupied, rather than put the other phone down, I chose to let go of the small hand holding mine for a moment, to try and beat the second ring. But before I could move phone-two even half-way towards my free ear, I felt it being smashed out of my hand by a surprisingly powerful force. I turned just in time to see the offending object hurtle into an unsuspecting bush and land, still ringing, deep inside its tangled roots. My eyes then came to rest on a familiar set of beautiful eyes fixed in the most defiant stare I had seen in the eight years 'to the day' that I'd been in love with them. That stare, accompanied by two little arms resting squarely on hips, stopped me in my tracks.

Gaining composure, I quickly ended the other call, promising to ring back shortly (I never did), and was about to unleash all my frustration and anger onto the most precious person in my life: then something incredible happened. As I opened my mouth, the distance between us was filled with the most honest, simple and heart-breaking truth I had heard then or since. "You are always on the phone Daddy. Why won't you play with me? Why won't you listen to me? Please spend time with me. It's my birthday. You are always on the phone Daddy; you are *always* on the phone."

It was only then that I noticed the park around me. It was like that moment in the movies where time stands still, and the central character breathes in the full reality of the moment – frozen in time. Some of the trees were losing their leaves, others had retained their deep and stunning green, the air was cold, but the sun shone brightly, and the park had attracted the usual array of dog walkers, parents with children, and people passing through. To my right, deep within a row of thick bushes, an electronic tone emitted, still calling for my attention. As the ringing stopped, I was hurtled back into the moment and time started again.

I turned the work phone to silent and put it in my pocket. Then we sat together on a bench and started enjoying what would turn out to be my favourite birthday of all time.

Now, I am not going to pretend I got everything right from that day onwards. The balance between work and family didn't become perfect overnight, and I didn't leave the phone in the bush as a punishment to myself. But things *did* change in my life. They changed at work and in my relationships with the people who matter the most to me. You see, for the first time as a business owner, I stopped to consider why I was there. Yes, I was hungry for the dizzy heights I had seen other people reach. And I also loved the adrenaline of being in demand, having my finger-on-the-pulse and being the one who made executive decisions to save the day. I was attracted to shiny new things, fast cars, and the trappings of the super-successful. And I cared what other people thought about me: my peers, my mentors and those who put me on the 'aspirational entrepreneur' pedestal. But all those things were inconsequential and somehow shallow when compared to what really mattered. The more I thought about what had happened in the park on that sunny October day, the clearer the picture became in my mind. Jace was the most important person in my life, but I was spending most of my time, attention, and endeavour, on building a business for me. The starkness of that statement alone didn't seem to balance itself out.

In the days that followed, I continued to dwell on these thoughts and have conversations with my team about reorganising my workload. I started to quantify some of my goals. I sought to discover what and who was most important in my life, the things that made me happy, how I liked to spend my downtime, places I would like to go and how my business could support that lifestyle instead of dominating it. It then occurred to me that every time I had heard a group of entrepreneurs ask questions like, "Who are you building the business for?" and "What is your driver?" or "Why are you working so hard?", they almost always answered the same way. They would give identical answers to the ones I had given. They would all claim they were working to build security for their families. Yet like me, almost every one of them, I knew, was guilty of neglecting time with their families to try and achieve that goal.

That day in the park is a day I will always remember because it was the day I decided not to pay lip service to my true ambitions any longer. And if you are a business owner reading this now, I urge you to look at what you are doing and ask if it is congruent with what you want. Not just a future 'want' you are striving to deliver as a result of your ten-year-plan to build security for your family; but whether what you want is in line with what your family wants today.

I deceived myself into thinking I was giving Jace what she wanted (my ego thought that was a new car, new toys and a flash dad). But when she stopped me in my tracks in that park on her eighth birthday and told me what she really wanted – it didn't include any of those things. If you are honestly doing what you do for your family, why not give them a chance to tell you exactly what they want? You might be surprised.

LESSON ONE

Work-life balance: the truth behind the cliché

The irony of the phone incident in the park that day was that as I stepped back from the 'busyness', the business began to step up. The more I allowed my team to take hold of their own reins, make independent decisions and have the freedom to do what they thought best, the better they performed. And as I handed over many of the administrative tasks and time-consuming involvement that had swamped my heart and mind, I found I was able to think bigger, smarter, 'business growing' thoughts. As you will learn in the next chapter of the book, there were elements of this approach that I hadn't mastered at the time, and the cost was dear. But there was no denying that less of my time in a sharper state of mind was significantly more effective.

There are two big problems with clichés. Their overuse seems to dampen their edge, and their offhand use often clouds the true meaning intended. The phrase 'work-life balance' began to appear in business literature and executive management conferences in the mid-1980s. Most trendy sounding mantras address a specific issue of the time, then die out or evolve to suit new ideas. The social structure of *this* time was starting to create more dual income families, single parents needing to work to survive, and women beginning to show the world they were the equal of any man in the workplace. So, there was a focus on finding ways for people to manage their working lives alongside the time and effort needed to manage life at home.

Today, for business owners in particular, the term has come to represent warding off the bombardment of work demands due to 24/7 connectivity. The truth is, trying to maintain a work-life balance is like trying to balance two balls on opposite ends of a stick with another larger ball as the fulcrum. It doesn't work. The options are; turn off your phone, tablet, and computer at five-thirty every evening and ignore the problems until nine the next day; or subliminally tell your family they will always come second. You cannot balance two things that are opposed to one another. You must change the equation. The only way to achieve harmony in your work and life is to construct your working life into a format that supports the life you want to live. I hope you can see the difference.

It means running your business more efficiently, not only so that it becomes more profitable, but also, so it leaves you with free time for the things you want to do. If you really want your family and your children to benefit from your hard work, you need to ensure they appreciate your involvement in their lives today, not just the finances you provide for them. Lonely riches are no substitute for loving, attentive and supportive parenting. Don't risk your children giving up on you like mine almost gave up on me. And, as I explained when I was relating *my* story, the benefit is that we eventually got to live the best of both worlds.

Please go and examine the focus of your efforts today. Ask yourself what work-life balance means to you. Are you, or have you ever been anywhere near, achieving it? Or is it time to look for a different strategy? What would have to happen in your business so you can give time to the things that matter most to you today, instead of risking everything in the pursuit of a pipedream that might be gone by the time you get there?

LESSON TWO

Recognise the difference between distractions or dangers

All those years ago, while I was hitting my tatty old tennis ball against a featureless wall and unknowingly teaching myself key lessons about life, I was risking my life. Today, what I was doing simply wouldn't be allowed, and either officials from the club, my parents, or the police would come and put a stop to such a dangerous hobby. You see, I was standing on one side of a road (albeit one of London's quieter streets) and hitting the ball across to the other so the wall could return it to me; being sure to avoid the curb on the other side. From time to time, my rallies would not be stopped by my lack of ability or a wicked slice from the corner of a brick; but by the act of sheer life preservation as a car drove by. I had to be constantly alert.

I suppose any onlooker would have observed a young lad going through some sort of imaginary pre-serve routine in honour or imitation of a sporting hero. I would stand there, ball in hand, bounce it once, look to the left to check for cars, bounce twice more, look to the right scanning for movement, and after a final bounce, breath deeply and serve underarm towards the wall. I then learned a skill very few tennis players, of any level, anywhere in the world had in their arsenal. If a fast-moving car came out of nowhere and sped across the court in the middle of a tournament match, Ash Taylor would probably be the sole survivor. Some things that go on around us in our lives are nothing more than distractions to be ignored. Others are danger signs or collisions that are a matter of life or serious injury. Learn to tell the difference.

The day my second mobile phone was sent flying into a bush by the force of a tiny but justifiably angry hand, I was sent a warning. To be fair, I didn't see danger signs or the collision coming, and I was fortunate that it didn't kill me. But it is no exaggeration to suggest that had I ignored that message for much longer it might have killed the most important relationship in my life.

There are dozens of distractions in our lives, many of them masquerading as important or urgent. But be careful the cry of 'wolf' from one does not stop you benefiting from another. We live in the age of online scams, computer viruses and hackers trying to steal our data. But occasionally the bank *does* send you a legitimate email. People *do* bombard us with sales calls, connection requests and offers to 'sign up now'. But some of the noise might actually help you. And every time you get in your car to drive, you will pass sign after sign that is trying to save your life and that of other road users. We become over familiar with many of these warnings; ignoring them, not seeing them; taking them for granted. And that is why there are so many tragic accidents on the roads each day.

Distractions or dangers?

As a business owner, your to-do list will be full of things you believe are your job and your responsibility. I would humbly suggest that many of them are no more than distractions. Managing your social media, bookkeeping, answering customer queries and other administrative tasks are keeping you from making a difference in your business. These are all distractions – don't do them. If you put aside time to think deeply about your business goals, devise a new marketing campaign that will generate sales, or educate yourself in a valuable new skill, I would suggest these are good uses of your time. But, if your phone rings or your email beeps during those 'value adding' moments, these are dangers that are sabotaging your business goals. I was fortunate that Aubrey Walk was a quiet road, and the cars were few and far between. But had it been a more popular route, it would have been far safer for me to move away and play somewhere else.

In your daily business life, you have got to identify the distractions and the dangers. Work out which ones can be ignored or deleted, what can be delegated or outsourced; what things deserve your attention; and look for the signs that are warning you of danger. Be honest with yourself as you make these assessments and deal with each new distraction or threat accordingly. Your business welfare and future lifestyle depend on it.

LESSON THREE

I'm better at playing doubles

As a species, human beings are community animals. I know some people think of themselves as loners, and there are certainly times when you need to shut yourself up in a noise free room to get your best work done. But for the best part, people feel most secure around their families, become creative around like-minded people, thrive when challenged by peers and long for good company. And in business, it is the same. You simply cannot go it alone and achieve any level of success. You will always be held back from achieving mastery, maximising delivery or keeping an eye on every important detail if you are trying to take on the world alone. You have to play as part of a team. And the good thing is, as a business owner, you get to choose who you play alongside.

When I played tennis, I was always better at doubles than on my own. And even as a singles player, it was when my match was contributing to a team event that I produced my best individual performances—just having my teammates courtside cheering, supporting and encouraging every shot made the difference for me. Even the physical science of playing doubles demonstrates its effectiveness because you can cover more ground. A singles court is twenty-seven feet wide while a doubles court is extended to the outer lines at thirty-six feet across. So, the court becomes one third bigger, but there are two of you in the team; therefore, each person covers only two thirds of the space required in singles. And, if you have ever watched a doubles match, you will see how the camaraderie, support and tactical encouragement is continuous, with a fist pump and a quiet word exchanged between every single point – win or lose. I loved playing doubles.

These days, my sport is golf, a famously individual sport where you play against your own level of ability and the inside of your mind. But my favourite versions of golf are team events where you stride out on a course and play alternate shots on each hole or simply double-up to submit a team score. I know dozens of people who are not golf players or particularly interested in the greatest sport on earth, at all. But who find themselves drawn to the drama and kingdom against kingdom struggle of the Ryder Cup. Teams and teamwork bring out the best in individuals and create results that are far bigger than the sum of the parts involved.

The other thing about teams is: people can play to their strengths and find support in the areas where they might let themselves down. You would think any football team fielding the greatest player to have ever graced a football field, Lionel Messi, would have a distinct advantage. But, at five-foot seven-inches, you wouldn't gain many benefits from playing him in goal. The more you play in a team, and the more you learn to rely on, utilise, discover and develop each other's strengths and weaknesses, the more effective your team will become.

Today, in my business, I run two types of team. My Mastermind Groups bring together a selection of individual business owners, from a variety of sectors, sizes of business and skillsets. There are typically five or six business owners per group, and we get together once a month then keep in touch regularly between meetings. The format is that we discuss the current challenges each business owner is facing, and we hold each other to account on commitments. We help clarify each other's direction, develop solutions, and provide support and friendships that help move us forward. In practice, it is like having a high-level, interactive strategy meeting with a team of brilliantly creative minds who are all as committed to your success as you are. And the more each person gets to know their team, understand the nuances and quirks of each other's business, engage with the real person and see behind their eyes, the more powerful the effect becomes. It truly is an amazing thing to watch the people in these groups develop, support one another, and achieve the life and business goals they have set their hearts on. In my business life, initiating these Mastermind Groups has been the best project I have ever been involved in.

My other team is the people who help me run my business. As I said before, I am not the perfect dad, or the best husband in the world – although I try every day to be the best I can in both those roles. Neither have I completely mastered the art of running a small business. But I do have one very strict and unbreakable rule. And it was born out of the events of that day in the park back in October 2011. I always put my home life first, and I never do any task in my business I am not qualified to do. Or, that I could pay someone else (less than I pay myself) to do for me. If there is one area of running a business I have mastered, it is that one. That day, I learned that my time is the most precious thing I have, and the primary purpose of my business is to allow me the time to enjoy the things in life that I love.

LESSON FOUR

Recognising strengths and weaknesses

I'm not sure I have ever met anyone who makes a mess of their life on purpose. But the tendency to trip yourself up within sight of the winning post, out of some unfounded sense of unworthiness, is more common than you would believe. However, the *deliberate* act of making mistakes, especially in that entrepreneurial breed known as the business owner, must surely be non-existent. The very definition of words like mistake or failure suggests an effort which didn't hit the target. And yet, we do all make mistakes. So, how do you go about reducing failings in your business life and cut out the things that are stopping you from reaching your potential?

The first stage of any transformation or change is always the same and always the hardest. Self-honesty and recognising that you have a weakness. Denial of a personal weakness sits directly in line with the mistake or failure itself – especially if it is recurrent and persistent. But if you want to grow a business that supports the lifestyle you want to live, you have to start by examining yourself first. Our weaknesses hold us back. And we can't let this happen when, fundamentally, we are at the helm of something we plan to develop and progress for the benefit of our entire lives and the lives of those we love. It needs to change. And the good news is that it *can* change.

So, work hard at getting past the most common failing in all entrepreneurs and business owners. For clarification, that is the one I just mentioned – admitting that you have weaknesses that need to be improved. Here are three of the most common weaknesses I come across in business leaders – and more importantly, how to fix them.

Micro-management

In the next chapter, I share in more detail the critical difference between delegation and abdication of responsibility. And I own up to how I learned this lesson the hard way. It was extremely painful, and it took a while, but I eventually recognised and corrected my weakness. Ultimately, you are the one responsible for the results in your business. If your business fails, you will have no one else to blame. But you are counting on the people who work for you to help deliver those results. That takes a lot of trust, and it is not easy. Most business owners fall into the default mode of handling this by micromanagement. They check up on employees three or four times a day, ask to be copied-in on emails, do work themselves instead of delegating and other 'big brother' management styles which only serve to tell the team you don't trust them.

If you want to grow your business, you need to utilise your team. You cannot do that if they feel (or you treat them like), they are still staff. So the best way to avoid this is to engage them in the conversation by asking for feedback and asking them what they need to help them achieve the goals you've set them. In the next lesson, I will talk about the dangers of losing control completely – there is a fine balance here – but you need to start by building trust. What you hear back might hurt your feelings, but you can't improve anything if you do not know it is a problem. The realisations that flooded my head and heart as I stood looking into those beautiful, angry and determined eyes in the park certainly hurt. But the actions I took after that day changed my life.

As a business owner, manager or leader, you need to work out what is important. Decide who is the best person to do any given task (you or someone else). And make sure there is a process (with a form of measuring the result) in place to ensure it gets done. If they need training, provide it. Or maybe they simply need the authority to make certain decisions themselves. So, set the parameters and allow them to take action. The more you involve good people in the bigger vision and goals of the business, the more they will get behind it and make it their own. My two caveats are; first, you are still in charge and must measure the results against the targets. And second, if you have the wrong people, change them quickly.

Closed to new ideas

This one is a real killer. Being closed-minded and stuck in your ways will cause your business to stagnate and eventually die. A business must move with the times and utilise the advances in technology, marketing trends and innovative thinking. As a business owner, a good use of your time is to spend it reading, researching, listening to podcasts, educating yourself and networking with other entrepreneurs. And if, after reading this book up to this point, your reaction to that statement is still, 'if only I had the time to do that' I would humbly suggest that you have not been absorbing what you are reading. You must be open to learning, and you cannot have a closed mind.

Be willing to try new things. If one of your team says something like, 'I've got an idea about how we can...' and you dismiss it in your head before they have even finished the sentence: that needs to change. I live for those moments in my business. I endeavour to pay for more of them. If for no other reason than it means my team, the people who are supporting me in building my business, care about making it better. What could be more exciting for a business owner than that? Listen to every new idea wherever it comes from. If it is from someone who works for you, or even a customer, show that you are listening by asking them questions. And always dig a little deeper before you decide against any idea. If there is one thing I have learned about inspiration, it is that it creates momentum and stimulates a diversity of new potential.

Are you open to an idea? How about blocking off thirty minutes of each working day, at a time that suits your schedule, where you set about learning something new? It could be reading blog posts from your competitors or leaders from other sectors who inspire you. You could try listening to a business podcast, signing up for some online training, actively inviting your team to talk to you about their ideas, or reading a book. Training your mind to be open and to explore opportunities and ideas has two major benefits. Firstly, you might just stumble across the one thing that supercharges your business into a whole new stratosphere. And secondly, your healthier, more active and less stressed brain will thank you for many years to come.

Insecurity

The two common failings I have already mentioned are probably caused by this last one. Self-belief is critical to running a business, especially if you are employing people. When things go wrong, everyone looks to you. They need to see someone who is strong and ready to take positive action. They need to believe in you. But how can they do that if you don't believe in yourself? Confidence, like inspiration, is both contagious and convincing.

But as business owners, we don't always feel confident, do we? And it is hard to maintain something you do not feel.

I have learned that confidence comes from two places. First, you need to have an abundance of knowledge, expertise, experience and understanding in the subject you want to show confidence in. If that is the sector you are running a business in, you have to study and learn as much about it as you can. Or, if it is a skill or ability that makes you good at what you do, you have to practise; continually hitting that ball against the wall, until you are the best you can possibly be. And then go and find a coach or mentor to make you even better. Perhaps it is that you struggle to focus. Or there is something, or someone, in your life making you doubt yourself; even though you are the very best at what you do already. The good news is that you can get help for that too. Asking for help is not a weakness – it is a sign that you are strong enough to identify hard truths.

The second-place confidence comes from is recognition of the facts. I often encourage my clients to write out a personal 'who am I?' statement – for their eyes only. The idea is that they put down on paper everything they represent as a business owner, as an expert in their field, as a provider of their service and as a person of value. It includes things like their years of experience in business and life, the things they have overcome to get to this point, their successes and achievements, how they have influenced and changed other people's lives and the hopes and dreams they have for the future. What this 'positive affirmation of self' does for the person is to force them to recognise their own value to their customers, their team and the people closest to them. It is very powerful, and I recommend that you try it for yourself.

There is so much to be said about recognising your strengths and weaknesses as a business owner. However, the first step is always being honest with yourself. This can be a painful wall to face but is a far more comfortable route to improvement than waiting for an eight-year-old to smash it into your attention on their birthday.

LESSON FIVE

Hard work does not have to be hard work

You will be familiar with the description 'being a busy fool'. Sadly, this is an accurate reflection of many small business owners and sits squarely alongside the similarly outdated saying: "As long as you are busy, that is the main thing." It is what people who have only ever been employees say when you describe how work is at the moment. And the worst way a business owner can respond to those well-meaning words is to nod in agreement. When someone says that to you it should set off an alarm in your mind that screams, 'stop running, upcoming wall fast approaching'.

Are you a business owner or the owner of a job? Yes, you might have set up a business and own that business (according to the name on the legal documents). But do you run a business, or do you do a job that pays you an income through a business entity? This is not a trick question. I want to challenge your thinking because, in practical terms, there is a clear distinction between being an owner and a doer. As entrepreneurs, we are passionate about what we do. Usually, we start doing it because we love it, and we're good at it. And we cannot resist getting hands-on and being involved in the thick of the action. I get this, because I have been there. And I also understand that when you are the best person for the job, it is incredibly difficult to step back.

During the next few paragraphs, I am going to refrain from using two words that might spring to your mind. See if you can guess what they are, and at the end of the chapter, I'll reveal what they are and why I never use them.

Business owners should run the companies that they own. They should see themselves as the CEO, the Managing Director, the Operations Manager; or a similar high-level position. Even as I write this, I can imagine some readers thinking, "But I am the only person in my business – I don't employ anyone". If that is you, I am talking to you as much, if not more, than to the owner who has people on the payroll. You have got to remember that you are the boss, the buck stops with you, and you cannot afford to be hands-on all the time. If you want to grow (and I admit that I am making an assumption here, so please bear with me for a sentence or two), you have got to find ways to reduce the time you spend on administration, social media, unscheduled phone calls and other low-value tasks. Someone else absolutely and unequivocally must start doing that work for you. And if your goals are not to grow, but to reduce the stress your business is causing you and your lifestyle, then the same solution applies.

As the owner of the business, your time and expertise is your company's most valuable asset. Let's imagine for a moment that your business is at a size today where you can afford to employ a Managing Director who is paid at the going market rate (plus car, pension, insurance and other benefits). Would you be happy if that person spent the majority of their paid time taking letters to the post office, answering the customer service hotline, reading social media posts, deleting spam emails, arranging their own meetings and occasionally picking and packing deliveries? No? So, why do *you* do it?

Managing a business is not about doing low-value tasks. Neither is it about sitting back and making everyone else work hard while you watch the money roll in. You need to work out which are the high-value tasks in your business. Identify what makes the business generate more income, run more efficiently, improve the service, increase its reputation, attract better customers and staff, and become more profitable. I do not know your business specifically, and it may be that you have expertise in certain areas which make it worth your time getting involved in administration or social media. If that is so, it must be a deliberate choice you make based on the value you deliver and the value of your time. But if there is anything at all that someone else can do as well as you for less than you pay yourself, you have got to pay them to do it for you. And it doesn't have to be someone you employ. When I present this idea to business owners, the most common objection is that no one else knows how to do it. My response is always the same. Create a process, write it down, then hand someone the job description – job done.

For most of my clients, the sort of things they view as high-value tasks include:

- High-level networking activities to identify new sales contacts and partners
- Driving smarter marketing campaigns and devising ways to promote the business
- Reviewing (not doing) the company finances to find efficiencies, funding, and control cash flow
- Managing the development of systems and processes to streamline operations
- Analysing, developing and improving business strategies and future direction
- Being the face of the business in marketing videos, campaigns and written materials
- Communication with the team to ensure adequate training, support and targets are maintained
- Doing elements of the 'work' that only the business owner can do (due to their unrivalled skill)

This is the work of a true business owner. And it is how they grow beyond that to become successful entrepreneurs. My definition of the entrepreneur is an evolution of the business owner: because they have created time in their busy working life to pursue new opportunities, identify the potential for growth or diversification; and they get to decide what they do next. These people work hard when choosing to, and they always work smart. Their businesses do not rely on them being there every single day, but they do need them to keep a steady, confident hand on the steering wheel. Entrepreneurs do not run into walls of stress, exhaustion or 'busyness'; they build walls of strength, support and mentorship.

Once you arrive in that position – and you can get there much sooner than you think – you can look to the future with your feet firmly planted in the present. And here is the big secret. You do not even need to employ people, in the traditional sense of the word, you just need to build a team around you. While it admittedly takes confidence, bravery and a well-plotted path or plan, you can still manage the biggest risk element (people) if you can lead a team.

So, the words that I refrained from using in this chapter were 'employee' and 'outsource' although I implied both. I refuse to use these words because

I do not think of anyone who helps me as someone I merely pay money to in return for a service. And neither do I want them to view our relationship that way. I am under no illusion that anyone will ever care about my business as much as I do. And I know they have their own hopes, dreams, goals and families too. But I do want them to care. So, anyone who becomes part of my team, whether they are on the payroll or operate independently, needs to meet that standard first. And the best way to gain that level of buy-in to an idea is to care, to give back and to be genuinely interested in what they want from the relationship too.

And if you direct all your hard work and effort into those strategies and relationships, you will have the potential for a business that will work hard for you. Let me give you an example of this in real terms. I wrote this book during the Summer of 2020, during the COVID-19 pandemic. The whole of the UK, and indeed the world, was under varying levels of lockdown restrictions. But, during this time, my team and I, (who did almost all the actual 'work'), also accomplished the following:

- Built two new websites
- Created a membership site
- Delivered 100s of hours of free support
- Launched a business podcast
- Undertook a complete rebrand
- Employed two new staff
- Started the search for an apprentice
- Wrote a business book
- And I took twenty-three weekdays off (100% out-of-the-business time – without my work phone)

LESSON SIX

Is your effort defeating your purpose?

As I write the final lesson of this chapter, I am very conscious that I may be repeating myself when I explain some of my thoughts and ideas. But the next paragraph is so important, and I want you to make sure you remember this if nothing else.

I was sacrificing time 'with' Jace 'for' Jace – but that was not what Jace wanted or needed. And the more I consider the poor judgment of how I spent my time back then, the more I realise it was because I did not think. Ironically, I did think about what I wanted my business to be and how much money I wanted it to make for me. Because I assumed that money would make me and everyone else I love happy. After all, that meant we could buy more stuff in the present and buy absolute security for the future. So, all my life plans were actually business plans because I believed that a successful business meant a successful life. And here is the point. A successful business can be the key to living a successful life if (and only if) you first work out what matters most in your life.

So here are the two thoughts I want to leave you with before we move into the next chapter and I reveal my biggest admission of failure. Because what I am about to tell you didn't fully sink in (even after the events I described in this chapter and the previous one about losing my sister) until I had built up and double-faulted my tennis empire.

Be absolutely certain about what you want from your life

If you skimmed over the vision board exercise I described in chapter one, please stop reading for a few hours, go back, and do it now. It will be the most valuable use of your time today. I promise you. You only live once, and if you are over forty (sorry if that sounds patronising to anyone younger), you don't have to think too hard to realise time is passing you by at an alarming rate. Remember, you have just 1,440 non-refundable, irretrievable, highly fluid and fragile minutes to spend each day. And even those of us who are acutely aware of that fact still let too many waste away into the ether of forgotten time. That sounds so dramatic – but I can't express how much this matters.

Look at your life today and split it into the categories and goals that are important to you. I gave you some examples in the vision board exercise, but you can describe your own. It is up to you, but they have to be things that get to the centre of your heart's desire. It could be family time, holidays, hobbies, learning to paint, writing a book, living abroad, living stress-free, growing your own vegetables, doing charity work. Whatever you know, deep down, will make your life a life worth living. Then, when you have done this, either through the exercise I described earlier or at the very least as a list on a piece of paper, ask yourself this question.

Are you satisfied or dissatisfied with these areas in your life?

Now I want to ask you a question, or more precisely, set you a challenge. If your lifestyle is not what you want it to be, **what would need to change for you to start living that life?** Now, to be clear here, I am under no illusion that every single person reading this book wants to live a totally altruistic life where they run a home for the poor or float up and down the Grand Union Canal on a longboat, enjoying the fresh morning sunshine each day, without a care in the world. It may be that you do want to live in a mansion in Dubai or Hawaii and run a multi-million-pound business that pays for your private jet and fleet of supercars. Either way, I believe the solution starts with deciding what you actually want your life to be – not what your peers and their view of the world tells you your business should be.

Once you are clear on your answers and have defined your goal, then, and only then, can you set about designing a business that will support them. And depending on those answers, there will be an equivalent level of bravery, risk, effort and support that you will need to find. But I do believe that regardless of the size, simplicity or giant ambition of your goals – the paths to reaching them are exactly the same. You need to utilise your walls: bounce off some of them, build on others and smash through any that stand in your way.

4

RUNNING BLIND

Hitting walls hurts – so keep your eyes, ears and mind open

My early obsession with tennis took me on the inevitable path of pursuing it as a career. And as I dozed off to sleep at night, I always stood on the baseline; battling warrior-like rallies against Sampras, Agassi and Hewitt. But in the cold light of day, I knew coaching was a more likely route to riches. Through my associations with Peter Hennessey Smith and others at the Campden Hill club, I landed various coaching roles; and I was determined to be the best I could be. I worked hard, put in more hours than anyone else, innovated my own training methods, and several of my students progressed to professional playing careers. Looking back, I am proud of my attitude, accolades and achievements. But some would cost me more than I could know at the time.

In 2005 the national governing body for tennis in the UK, the Lawn Tennis Association (LTA), approached me with a development role in Oxfordshire and Devon. I moved from London to Abingdon, and my job description was straightforward: make a difference to the tennis potential coming out of this area of the country. For a young, eager and ambitious mind like mine, there was no better opportunity in the world. So, I started building a structure and developing a programme with the resources available and a few I poached from elsewhere. I could see my route to world domination beginning to take shape.

My plan included training and developing the skills of my coaches and setting up mentoring schemes so clubs could work closer with schools in the area and with each other. Another focus was to build a supportive community among the coaches and the volunteers in the area because if there was one thing Peter had shown me it was that relationships matter. There was, of course, a budget to work within, so I set up a facilities department to oversee the redevelopment of clubhouses, new courts and floodlights. In one area of the two counties, we built a new clubhouse, with facilities, from scratch. In my mind, the ultimate goal was simple: make the game easily accessible to as many people as possible. I figured that the more people were happily playing the game, the quicker all the other objectives would be reached and my name would soon be in lights. While I was guilty of a lot of mistakes and misplaced priorities in those days, that strategy, at least, was a sound one and has served me well ever since. Identify the one thing that will make the most significant difference to everything else and aim the majority of your resources in that direction.

Over the following 18 months, the young me could not imagine a better lifestyle. I was living my dream (well one version of it anyway), and nothing could stand in my way. From every angle, I was the epitome of the mantra, 'find a job you enjoy doing, and you will never have to work a day in your life'. More than that, though, I felt I was actually making a difference, and the numbers supported it. When I took over, there was one LTA Level 5 qualified coach in the whole of Oxfordshire, and by the time I left, we had eight. And the infrastructure was there to support them too. We had mentoring schemes, exceptional facilities, funding, quality tennis players coming through; and growing queues at the doors. From players who had nowhere to play, through to newcomers who had never dreamed they would be able to; we had found them a home.

Then something changed in the upper echelons of the LTA. A high-flying new boss had taken the top job and decided they needed to make their mark. As is often the case in large organisations, a person who had never set foot on a tennis court in Oxfordshire, whose degree in business management didn't include a paper on developing a promising backhand, and who hadn't witnessed 18 months of progression, decided to change things.

When my entire team were forced to reapply for their jobs, with six months' probation, it wasn't just the lack of appreciation we all felt. For me, it was also the freedom to follow my creativity. Knowing I was making a difference but being replaced by a jobsworth who ripped out my heart and filled it with paperwork and ticking boxes. For a year, I begrudgingly ticked those boxes, tried to be as creative as I could within the rules, and moved from loving life and work to hating my job. Finally, I could take no more and set off on a quest to rediscover what I had glimpsed for the briefest moment at the LTA – a lifestyle business.

Ash Taylor Tennis was incorporated in November 2009, and I had a big vision of UK-wide, David Lloyd-style influence and recognition. The basic idea and business model were simple. Small clubs in rural areas had very few opportunities to access quality coaching for their members; if any at all. That meant these clubs were little more than a court hire facility and social centre for the community, and prospects for development or investment were limited.

Meanwhile, there were freelance coaches out there who were unable to find even five or six hours work a week at clubs and were struggling to make ends meet. I saw how two problems could become a solution for each other (basically the essence of any successful business) and devised a programme to make those two ends meet. In addition to that, I adapted the tried, tested and successful mentoring and training schemes I had developed at the LTA to ensure a consistent standard of training across all the clubs. Although I didn't fully appreciate it at the time, this element of the business was a game-changer in ensuring the company's reputation and turnover grew.

My target market for coaches was the 'young, enthusiastic, and newly qualified'. The ones I could train and mentor in my style. I would then place them in rotating roles with two or three clubs each. This meant the programmes could be flexible and adapt to the needs of each club as I could supply almost any contract size. I also had access to a hungry workforce who were being offered three or four times the hours an independent coach received. And to be sure I kept my supply lines flowing, I opened a sister company; Ash Taylor Education; to train new coaches from scratch in the way that I wanted them to work. This gave me a pool of recruits from which I could hand-pick the best of class in advance and offer them a job.

Once again, I had found my dream scenario. And in the 18-months from January 2011 to the middle of 2012 the business grew from £30,000 per year to £300,000. I was flying. I will cover more of the innovative and creative ideas that helped achieve this rapid increase in turnover later. But for now, I want to explain how the illusions of outward success often blind you.

You don't see the gigantic wall into which you are about to smash. Running a business with your eyes closed, especially one that was accelerating as fast as mine, is a devastating crash waiting to happen. And in this one, too many people got hurt.

You see, I knew exactly what it took to turn a good coach into an outstanding one. I had designed quality mentoring and coaching programmes to improve players' games and attract people to the sport. I could generate funding applications, improve facilities, recruit good people, build communities and run successful marketing campaigns. But I had no idea how to run a business. And trust me, there is a massive difference.

Michael Gerber's landscape-defining book, The E-Myth, is one of the most impactful books I have ever read. It is the type of book that smacks you in the face and says, 'wake up, you idiot'. But only if you are reading it at the right time and you are open to its wisdom. The first time I read it, I wasn't. Needless to say, I've studied it in great detail since.

For a long time after I lost the business, all my reasons and excuses for the failure were aimed at what other people did and didn't do. It is only more recently, with the benefit of clearer vision and hindsight, that I have reflected on the real reason for its demise. I failed to see the aforementioned wall because it is hard to see walls if your head is buried up to its neck in the sand, or you are blindly distracted by all the busyness of doing business.

My two biggest problems revolved around money or, more specifically, getting cash into the business. You may think that is an incredibly obvious area to overlook for a business owner. But you would be stunned at just how many people avoid the uncomfortable issue of money altogether and how the majority of business owners have less than a nursery school understanding of their business numbers.

Our first problem was credit control. Also known as getting customers to pay on time. In truth 'on time' wasn't even the real issue, it was that we gave them too long to pay in the first place and then let them get away with delaying transferring the cash as long as they could. The thought of turning away a child because their parents hadn't paid for two or three months never even occurred to my customer-focused, hyper-positive team. I think some customers felt like I was running a charity (and in hindsight, I may as well have been). The second issue was the cyclical nature of the business. This was slightly different because it wasn't as though I could control the ebbs and flows of weather and seasonal preferences. But I should have managed its effects more efficiently.

To give you an example of the challenges we faced, on one record-breaking day at the end of February 2012, I watched with a huge smile on my face as £42,000 landed in the business account. Then during the entire month of November that same year, the takings were around £400. Of course, I could see we had money in the bank, but I didn't understand the impact of the varying levels of income over the long term. This caused havoc with the cash flow in the business, and when the coaches needed paying monthly, but many of the schools would pay three months later, it didn't help ease the situation.

Finally, there was the issue of placing too much trust in other people and my tendency to assume the best of everyone. As I said before: initially, I blamed the company's demise on the people who I believed had abused my trust. But the truth is, if I had understood my numbers, trust would have been an equation I could interrogate as accurately as I could have controlled my cash flow. Instead of raging, accusing and blaming, I could have presented facts, requested answers and – most importantly of all – foreseen the problem. I have learned my lesson, and because I now take full and total responsibility for the failure of my business, I am not even going to soil these pages with details of how I think certain people stole from and deceived me.

It was 5th December 2013 when I pressed the button and sent the last official email to tell the world that Ash Taylor Tennis had lost in the final set of a five set thriller, having thrown away several set-points in the third. The preceding months saw the first tears I had cried since my sister died, and my first visit to the psychiatrist's couch. My thoughts constantly moved between the people I had let down, the shame of being viewed a failure, and wondering what people would say about me behind my back. My struggle to fight, and stubborn refusal to see what was inevitable eventually cost my house, a sizeable chunk of my own money and left me significantly in debt to my mum. I was financially, physically, emotionally, mentally and professionally wrecked – and then I sighed with relief.

I sighed with relief because the weight had become unbearable. I had tried everything to save the business; cutbacks, borrowing, deals, counter-deals, buyouts, pleading and partnerships. But in the end, the people issues, money matters and abundance of unpleasantness seeping through the woodwork was too much. And sometimes cutting your losses, picking up the pieces and packing up the lessons to be learned, is the only way to get around the foreboding shadow of a wall.

LESSON ONE

The importance of failure

Failing in life and business is probably the best thing that can ever happen to you. Of course, I'm not suggesting it should be part of your business plan, or you strategically set out to self-sabotage your efforts just as you are about to cross the victory line. If you can go through your entire business life and never make a mistake or fail at anything, good luck to you – where can I buy your book? What I mean is that when you fail, and you inevitably will, you should embrace the opportunity, learn from it, and become better equipped for the next time (which is just as inevitable).

You may be familiar with the Japanese proverb 'Fall down seven times: stand up eight'. This attitude is so apt for business owners because circumstance, naivety or your own pride will trip you up sooner or later. Sorry if that sounds like pessimism. If you think that please reread these first few paragraphs. What I'm saying is that hardship makes you stronger in the long run and if you take it on with the right attitude you will come out the other side faster and more likely to hear and apply the lessons it teaches you.

Failure is an integral part of life and business success. So, learn from it and, as the proverb advises, stand up again. Keep going. The chances are you do not remember learning to ride your bicycle. But I can tell you this for a fact: you would have fallen off a few times in the process. Today, however, you can ride with very little chance of hitting the deck and without paying much attention to the skill required. Similar scenarios will have applied when you learned to drive a car, started swimming, closed your first deal, or stood up in front of a roomful of business owners and explained what you do. We learn every time we do something new, and we rarely get things right the first time. But eventually, we become so proficient (maybe not the public speaking for some people) that what was once a trial is now something that helps generate income for our business. And it is the fact that we failed at the beginning that makes us more adept at those things now.

The brilliant Elon Musk (owner of Tesla and SpaceX) believes you should always try something if it is important enough – even if there is a strong chance you could fail. Among his foundation philosophies is a belief that failure is worth it to make progress and that '... if you are not failing, you are not innovating enough'. Love him or loath him, if you look into Musk's back story, you see a man who will stop at nothing to pursue the most ambitious dreams on the planet. Neither cost, opposition nor fear of failure is going to stop him pursuing his desire to spend his final years living and innovating in one of the super-hotels he is planning to build on Mars. And, looking at his track record, who is to say he won't achieve that goal?

The thing about accepting failure as part of the process of finding success is that you no longer need to fear it. Yes, it can be disheartening and make you question what you are doing. Indeed, it should make you ask what, why and how you are going about your business – but it shouldn't ever stop you moving forward. Failure is not failure; it is part of the process of turning a business owner into a successful entrepreneur.

Tackle self-induced failure first

I am not a psychologist, but I spend most of my business life these days working with people. So, I know that the way you think and feel combined with what you choose to believe about the world and yourself is the single biggest factor in how successful you will become. I also know, from working with hundreds of business owners and budding entrepreneurs over the years, that it is the single biggest problem they face.

Technically, in the literal sense, I am not a business coach either, even though that's my title. In my years as a tennis coach, there was not a single day that I coached a tennis ball or a tennis racket. I only ever focused on the player. I could teach them how to hold the racket, stand correctly, strike the ball cleanly; and dozens of other technical nuances of the game. But mostly, I worked with the mind of the person holding the racket and hitting the ball. I worked with their presence in the moment, their determination to win and attitude to defeat. Business owners are no different to tennis players or sports people in any other field. Yes, technical ability, strength and speed are essential. But what is going on in the mind of the individual is what matters most. And more often than not, that determines the winner of any game. Most failure occurs when players defeat themselves before the game even starts.

There are so many external challenges facing today's small business owners and entrepreneurs. Financial restraints, keeping up with technology, people issues, mastering the mysteries of marketing and dozens of other things that can trip you up or cause you to fail. Often it is hard to control what comes at us from outside. But there is one area we can learn fast and make every effort to manage. One thing a business owner has total control over and must take full responsibility for. Themselves.

Don't beat yourself up if you let yourself down. But do apply yourself to learning from the failure and making yourself better able to stand firm the next time.

LESSON TWO

You have got to keep score

Can you imagine two topflight professional football teams battling it out for 90-minutes and no one keeping a note of the score? What would be the point? Or, imagine three hours of intense baseline rallies, cross-court passes and athletic drives to rescue lost points; without a single ace, love or game point being registered. Where would the drama, the prize or the draw for fee-paying crowds be for any sport played like that? To make it worthwhile, you simply have to keep score. And yet, in far too many businesses, the owners choose not to follow their numbers: the one thing which ultimately tells them if they are winning or losing the game. Another scenario that would remove the competitive edge and purpose from a game would be if the players didn't understand the scoring system. Imagine a cricketer being unaware that a boundary without a bounce gave him a maximum six points. Or if the greatest snooker player on earth had not been told the difference in score between potting a black or yellow ball. Maybe there would still be a level of thrill in a well-executed passing shot or brave defensive tackle, but the score is the thing that matters most. Ask any fan what they would prefer, points on the board or valiant defeat? You'll soon get the picture.

Business is no different. The stakes are just as high, and the results should be personal. Not only do you need to know what your numbers are; you must understand what they mean, where to find them and, most importantly of all, how to manage or affect them. If you are behind in a game, you must know the deficit you need to make up. Only then can you devise a strategy or plan of attack to rescue the situation and pull off a heroic second-half comeback. How can you do this in your business if you don't even know you are losing money? And please don't fall into the trap of thinking that making sales always means your business is profitable. These numbers are related, yes, but are never the same thing. If you are five-two down in a tennis set, you know you have to win the next three games in a row to have any chance of winning that set. There are no other options. Likewise, in the sport of business, where winning is everything, you need to know if your cash reserves will only keep you going for another two months. Only with that clarity can you be sure that you must win another contract *and* get the deposit paid for you to survive. The numbers should determine every business decision you make. And if you feel self-conscious or greedy because you care about the money, simply view your business numbers as 'keeping score' rather than cash. I like to use phrases like "let's look at the business commercials" when negotiating the costs within my business.

The playground matters

There is a saying, 'It is not the winning, but the taking part that counts'. This is complete rubbish. Of course winning counts – why take part otherwise? I'm not suggesting you should be a bad loser, throw your toys out of your pram whenever your plans fail, or that you set out to win at all cost (fair or foul). But even children playing in a playground should care if they win or lose, and always do their best to achieve the former. You need to experience losing so you can learn how to win. And when you lose, it should hurt. But if you don't *want* to win, the lesson of losing is lost. Life is not fair, and sometimes your best efforts are not good enough. But that doesn't mean you should give up or try something else. A winning mentality means working harder, creating a better strategy, and having another go.

There are key numbers you need to know, understand and control in your business if you want to win. This is not a book about accountancy; neither is it a book about running a business. It is about managing *you* as the business owner and helping you to not only overcome the obstacles in front of you but learn from the experience also. Winning and losing is all part of the game, but some elements of a business are critical. Losing control of your business numbers is not something you can easily recover from. So, without giving you an accountancy lesson, it would be remiss of me not to encourage you to become knowledgeable about the following:

- **Breakeven number** - what is the minimum amount of revenue you need to generate to cover all the outgoings in your business? That includes paying your staff and yourself.
- **Cash flow** - you need to know exactly how much cash you have in your account today; and what you expect to have 10 days from now, 30 days, 60 days and 100 days.

- **Margins** - it is critical you understand the difference between gross and net profit and, as a consequence, the compound effect of increasing your prices, offering discounts or adjusting the cost of delivering your products and services.

There are, of course, dozens of essential concepts to understand and master as a business owner. But after reading this book, if one thing you do is to book an appointment with your accountant to find out more; I will be satisfied that it was worth writing. And if your accountant looks at you blankly, or asks why you want to know – please, please, please sack them and find one that understands.

As I said, this is not a book about business finance, and I am not an accountant. But I have been a business owner who likes shiny new things and rewarding himself for wins, record months and deceptively healthy-looking bank balances. I know what it is like to think you are winning when your wall has been built on fragile ground. So, here is my final piece of financial advice. Instead of committing to a new office on a two-year contract, buying a new car or booking that dream holiday because you've just hit your third month of record sales – do this. Having worked out your breakeven number (the overhead costs to run the business), put aside enough to cover that for a month. Then set new SMART targets to build that up to three months, six months and one year. After that, you can call yourself a successful business owner and treat yourself to the rewards you so thoroughly and richly deserve.

LESSON THREE

Cross the line and stay there

What type of person are you? In chapter one, we looked at the idea that a wall is made up of lots of bricks; each one is influencing the strength of the wall around it. Like the people in your life, the influences that you surround yourself with will have a significant impact on the person you become. The most important brick in your wall, however, is you. How you manage *you* and the sort of person you are will ultimately determine the kind of people you attract and whether they will want to be a part of your team.

If you want to succeed in the games of life and business, the first thing you need to do is learn to get the ball over the net. Get the basics right, and from there, the rest will follow. So, here is a little exercise to determine which side of the line you sit and how to make sure you stay on the right side.

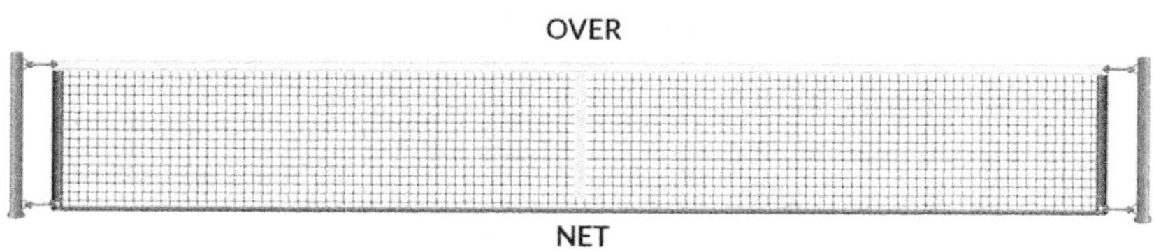

- **Ownership:** you accept responsibility for everything that happens in your life and business
- **Vision:** you regularly set clear SMART goals that fulfil your today and motivate you for tomorrow
- **Expertise:** you commit to understanding the critical aspects of running a business (finance, people, marketing etc.)
- **Resilience:** you remember to be grateful when things go wrong; stand firm, lean on your wall and move on

----

- **Negativity:** you have a pessimistic outlook and let negativity dictate your mood and your actions
- **Excuses:** you make excuses; blaming others for your mistakes rather than owning them and learning from them
- **Timidity:** you hide behind your wall and settle for your 'lot' in life; you don't search for opportunities and take them

Go through each of the words and definitions above the net and see how you measure up each day. The first and fourth words (ownership and resilience) are states of mind you need to adopt, while the second and third words (vision and expertise) are strategies and activities you should work into your life.

Then, look at the three words below the net. Every time you find yourself playing this sort of approach shot, you need to count it as a point dropped – an unforced error. If you continually fail to achieve results in your business and life, it will undoubtedly be because these behaviours are present. From this day onwards, every time you notice yourself behaving this way take time out, accept that you might have thrown the game that day, and start the next day with an ace.

LESSON FOUR

Look out for bright lights in the darkness

Although a quote attributed to many people, as a lover of golf, I am going to go with Gary Player's version. "It is funny how the more I practice, the luckier I get." As I said earlier in the book, with my sister's life being cut short so tragically, I do not believe there is a greater purpose out there for everything. But, if you can find it within yourself to remain positive, build on what you know for sure, and keep your eyes open, there will always be opportunities. It is when you lose hope and let your head and vision fall that great things pass you by.

I am so thankful that within the sigh of relief that came out when I closed the door on my business, I recognised I still had something of value to give. Perhaps that moment was when I leaned on my wall most of all and took strength from my mountain of previous experiences. Whatever it was, I had my eyes open, and some of Gary Player's 'luck' came my way instantly and in abundance.

On 13th December 2013, I booked a weekend away on my own at a mindfulness retreat in Wales. And as I closed the door on Ash Taylor Tennis forever, and headed west along the M4, I had no idea how quickly I would find a new door – and not one I was expecting. You see, to add to the emotional turmoil of losing my business, I had also been battling through the breakup of a long-term relationship and enforced time apart from my daughter, Jace. So, when I met a wonderful person called Kay during that first day of mindfulness and escape from the world, the last thing I had considered was the possibility of a new relationship. We were both there to deal with a past that we wanted to forget. To clear out the pain, gather the lessons learned and start new chapters. We got on from day one, but I had no idea that days two, three and every single one since would bring such wall-like strength, friendship and happiness. We got married on 15th June 2019, to put the seal on what had been five years of the most loving partnership I could have possibly dreamed of – thank you, Kay.

Shortly after returning from the retreat, one of my ex-rivals in the tennis coaching world called and asked how I was doing. I'd known Gary Drake for many years, and the previous year, when I first recognised (albeit reluctantly) that the business might be in trouble, I had offered him the chance to buy me out. He spent a fair bit of time looking into my numbers, clearly with a smarter view than mine at the time, and decided it wasn't viable. I don't know if he had heard on the grapevine that my whole life had come crashing down around me, or if it really was a call out of the blue, but his intention was genuine for sure. And by the end of that call, he had offered me a job. He didn't need me, as he certainly had resources within his team, but he paid me a six-month retainer to go into one of his clubs and help turn it around. This life-saving, simple act of kindness; from someone who I had previously seen as a rival; outshone the selfishness of those who were supposed to be on my side. The breathing space Gary gave me was enough for me to pick myself up and start to find my stride again.

Shortly after, I was at a two-day entrepreneurs' conference that I had spent hundreds of pounds to attend (having booked it while still under the illusion I was a successful business owner). Ironically, I had a reputation for being among the super-successful within this group, so I was feeling like a serious fraud – especially as I was now an employee, not a business owner. The evening after the first day, I went for a walk and stopped on a bridge, sending my thoughts aimlessly across the streets of Birmingham. I was still questioning my right to be at that conference and wondering how I was going to get out of the mess I was in. Then, seemingly from nowhere, a guy approached me and asked if I was Ash Taylor. It was Dan Harrison, a brilliant WordPress Developer who was also attending the conference, looking to strengthen his wall. He was putting together a peer-driven mastermind group to meet once a month for moral support. Its purpose would be to share experiences and support and answer each other's business questions or problems. Once again, in my darkest hour, an opportunity had come knocking. And I said, 'yes please'.

Many other amazing things happened around that time. But here is the thing – I don't believe they were my luck turning – I think that circumstance had opened my eyes to opportunity.

When you are at your lowest point, remember to look up

It may be that some people are just so unlucky they go through an entire lifetime without a single opportunity ever crossing their path; although I doubt it. It is like that football match where every decision goes against you, the woodwork starts playing like a second goalkeeper in the opposition's net, and you lose one-nil despite having 25 shots on target and 73% of the possession. There are anguished cries from the stands, as the faithful bemoan their bad luck, and the referee is taunted for bias and blindness in equal measure. But every fan, in more honest and reflective moments, also knows these games level themselves out over the course of the season.

Life is the same, and it is when you are at your lowest ebb that it is most important to look up. I am not saying I am grateful that I lost my business in the way I did. But maybe if I hadn't, I would not have stumbled across my rock, Kay. And people like Dan, Gary and others might not be part of my wall today. I will never know what could have been, but I am certain I would not have stumbled across such gems if I had kept my head down in the dumps.

LESSON FIVE

Delegate does not mean abdicate

I have talked about the importance of both understanding and then taking action based on your business numbers. And I have been very open that my failure to do so was the primary reason I lost my business. Statistically, that should come as no surprise. The main reason the majority of companies fail in the first few years is down to poor money management. But if I had to summarise how I lost my business in one sentence, it would be this: I misunderstood the word 'delegate'.

There is a deep irony behind my misunderstanding of this word because most business owners are incredibly poor at delegating – but I wasn't. It is simply not in the nature of most entrepreneurs to let go of anything and is based on their unshakeable belief that they can do things better than anyone. When the business means everything to them, and they are working eighty-hours a week to ensure its success, they find it hard to trust anyone else. Watching their staff clock off on-the-dot of their forty-hour shifts and not looking back as they ease into their weekends doesn't help the trust factor much either. Unsurprisingly, control-obsessed business owners believe they are the only one who actually cares about the success of the business. If poor cash management is the biggest killer of businesses, then poor delegation skills are undoubtedly the biggest killer of business owners.

Delegating, however, was not a problem for me. I had learned from people like Peter, Hugh and Al at Campden Hill Lawn Tennis Club that putting trust in other people was incredibly powerful. As I took on and started to understand the scope of the LTA role, I realised it was far too big a project for one person to manage. My life and work experiences, and my universal obsession with sport, had taught me the clear advantages of a strong team working together. And teamwork, in all its forms, relies on allowing other people to take responsibility for their own tasks. So, as I've said, delegating was never an issue for me. I relished the ability I had developed to build trust, single-mindedness and shared goals in my teams. I loved being busy managing everyone else and keeping their morale and strategic focus on track.

But when I started delegating responsibilities at Ash Taylor Tennis, I failed to grasp one crucial thing. At every tennis club I had worked as a coach, whenever I had represented a team in a tennis tournament, and in the role where I was able to make a difference across two counties in the South West of England, I wasn't actually in charge. People often reported to me, but ultimately, I passed my report further up the line to the place where the buck stops.

As a business owner, you must delegate – absolutely and unequivocally – or you will never grow your business beyond a glorified job. But you are still responsible for every single thing that happens within your business. And if you do not know what is happening, you have abdicated your responsibility. How do you know if you are winning or losing when you do not know how to read the game? Going back to my keeping the score analogy a few chapters back: sometimes you go in at half time, and the score is nil-nil, but you still know you are winning because, as the leader, you can see all the good things your team are doing. The chances they are creating and the commitment they have to each other and the cause. In that scenario, your team talk consists of nothing more than "well-done team, keep doing what you are doing, and we will take all three points today". But you can only say that if you can see how they are performing – otherwise you are just like any other spectator and the result is purely down to the team.

Taking responsibility

Trust is essential in business, but not as essential as certainty. In my business, I made the mistake of trusting people without ever checking they were worthy of it. And we've established delegation is essential – but not as essential as managing those you are delegating to. I assumed everyone else would always be as diligent and committed to achieving my goals as I was. Vision and direction are fundamental building blocks of any successful business owner's toolbox. But their number one goal should be to ensure their team understand the direction they should all be facing.

These are the four basic building blocks of delegation and managing responsibility for a business owner:

1. Do the work that only you can do, and which brings the most value to you and the business
2. Delegate every role that costs less than your hourly rate
3. Ensure there is a clear process in place for the delegated roles (including reporting and expectations)
4. Meet with your team regularly to measure, encourage and keep their efforts in line with your goals

Delegation of work is not an abdication of responsibility. It is releasing you from the stress and time cost of a task so you can effectively manage the bigger picture and get more done.

LESSON SIX

You cannot teach tennis from a book

So far, in this chapter, I have talked about the pitfalls and lessons I learned from losing my business. If the wall I hit my ball against as a child represented an early coach, and the wall I slammed into when my sister died was one that stopped me in my tracks, this one became a true foundation for what I did next. This is the wall that stood in my path, but which I eventually climbed and stood upon. It enabled me to stop and scan the horizon; see where I was going, and do so with a head and heart full of hard-won experience. Ultimately, this chapter was about learning from failure and being strong enough to get up and carry on.

But getting it wrong is not the only way to learn. It is essential that you recognise the things you do right as well. Celebrate them and make sure they remain part of your armoury. After all, I did grow my business from £30,000 to £300,000 in around 18 months so I must have done something right. To finish this chapter, I am going to share some of my wins from that period with you.

An unplayable passing shot

My best performing piece of marketing (to this day) came in the form of five DVD players. (For younger readers, a DVD player was needed to play thin discs loaded with data. In particular, films. This was before Netflix changed the movie world forever). At one of my early meetings in a Mastermind Group, somebody told me that all that was needed was 'a packet of stamps and a pair of brass balls'. At the time, I had been sending the same bland flyers and letters every other coaching company sent, and to the same 5,000 tennis clubs. During that same meeting, I was also challenged to name which clubs I would actually like to work with. To which I named the five I considered would be the cream of the crop for my business.

So, after that meeting, I went to Dixons and purchased five DVD players. When I got home, I started scripting and planning the best promotional video for Ash Taylor Tennis I could. The critical thing to say here is that the video was good quality, well-scripted, explained precisely why our offer would be so good for the club receiving it; and had a strong call to action at the end. But it wasn't the video that made the promotion work so well. It was the DVD players and the uniqueness of the approach. We stood out, not because of what we said but because of what we did. How we handled our marketing spoke volumes about how we would look after our customers.

With my video made and recorded onto five DVDs, I placed one inside each of the DVD players and posted them to the five clubs I had singled out as my ideal clients, along with the carefully crafted sales letter. And within each package, I placed the crème de la crème of unplayable passing shots. A post-it note from my daughter which read: 'When you have finished watching my daddy's video, please can you send back my DVD player?' Every single one of those clubs called me, and four of them became clients. All five DVD players were returned to us, and I sent three of them to the next 'ideal clients' on my list. Two of those also became clients. And the two remaining DVD players? I gave them to Jace and her friend.

Feeding a hungry crowd

There is a saying that 'a poor product, well-marketed, will always outsell a good product, badly marketed' and that could not be truer in the 'first sale' world. But the only way to maintain sales and popularity is to deliver a great product. Such was the level of service, community and quality we created in the business that, at its peak, we had 1,200 children in our clubs wearing t-shirts bearing my name. We were operating in over forty schools, and I had created opportunities for dozens of coaches, including two full-time community coaches. I was making a difference.

Seeing new opportunities

At one point, we spotted there was a gap in our supply chain. So we set up Ash Taylor Education: taking enthusiastic sixteen-year-olds, training them, then putting them alongside professional coaches and giving them a structure and roadmap to find their way into a job. In business, you must identify weaknesses in your supply lines, that's crucial. And for us, in that circumstance, the best solution was to fill the gap ourselves.

Fine-tuning my game

In the last chapter, I talked about how I had unknowingly abdicated responsibility, but that I was good at delegating. Well, here is the thing. I got into this business because I had recognised I was a good tennis coach. But, while running Ash Taylor Tennis, I rarely did any coaching at all. My focus was on making sure my coaches were doing a great job on the court; that every child, parent and school loved what we were doing; and that we kept winning business because we had the best clubs around. As a business owner, I spent my time fine-tuning my game as a marketer and service provider. Unfortunately, I learned other aspects of running a business too late, but that shouldn't take away from the huge success we achieved within that time.

Award-winning business

As a result of the positive things we did within Ash Taylor Tennis during those 18 months of exponential growth, the business was recognised for a range of awards. We were voted the second most loved coaching business in the UK in 2011 and, in December 2012, I was awarded The Entrepreneurs Circle 'Entrepreneur of the Year' for the Thames Valley area.

I have finished this chapter with a few highlights because it is important to recognise and celebrate your wins while you are building walls to lean on and support your growth. You cannot teach everything from a textbook; you need to be out there living it, doing it, winning, losing and getting stronger each time. Hitting walls is all about learning from your experiences and from becoming a better business owner, manager, marketer, mentor, coach and person. You have to live through the highs and the lows, accept them for what they are, always taking the good from whatever happens. Not every situation will be good, but there is usually a good lesson to learn.

5

MENTAL STRENGTH

The doctor called it depression

I have left this wall until last because the previous four were all scenes from my past. This one is the amalgamation of the various walls and barriers I have created for myself or have been thrown in my way throughout my life. The difference with this one is that it still lives with me today, and I still need to negotiate my way through its dark shadow from time to time. I don't know how it started exactly, but I want to tell you the story of one of the possible early trigger points.

One, two, three, four, five, miss... But I didn't miss this time. I landed squarely in the shit. Literally.

You know those moments in time that stick vividly in your memory for the rest of your life; big, bold and as real as the day they happened? This one took place a few years before the long days of hitting a tatty old tennis ball against a wall became an intrinsic part of my future. But it is as powerful in terms of events that influenced the person I became as those repeated swings against the wall of number nine, Aubrey Walk, W8.

The incident itself took less than five seconds of my life, but it changed everything. And it is, in part, responsible for the person I still become on some days; days where I usually try and hide from the world. For a long time, I wasn't proud of that person, and I didn't understand or recognise myself within him. I would go as far as to say I hated 'me' whenever that part of my character appeared. It is different now, and I've learned to manage myself far better. But it made for many very scary times in my life, I can tell you. The mind can be a minefield of emotions, falsehoods and insecurities if you don't work hard at allowing gratitude and positivity to take the controlling share of the chaos.

I was having the best afternoon ever. And what is odd, although maybe not so odd when you consider the impact the later actions of that day had on my future, I can remember every moment. It was a warm day; we were playing football on a makeshift pitch, and I took the starring role as one of my heroes, David Bardsley. I was awesome. We all were in our own mind's eye. But I was the only one who scored a hat-trick that afternoon.

We alternated between giggling uncontrollably like only young boys can (and only up to a certain age as after that giggling is for 'girls only' of course) and screwing our faces in concentration under the sheer responsibility when the ball was 'ours'. The sun was hot on our backs as we darted around with purpose, unafraid of injury and probably looking like a bunch of mini, human bumper cars. Just excited to be boys.

When the final whistle blew, and dinner beckoned, like any over-excited six-year-old, I burst through the door looking for someone to tell of my impressive goals between the jumpers. But I didn't realise I was bringing literal evidence of the day in with me. Along with that hot, sweaty kid's exuberance, the family were treated to a sticky mess and a distinct smell. A very nasty smell: you know the one I mean. It came in on the bottom of my shoe, and I shared it generously throughout every room in the flat before anyone could stop me. The entrance when I came through the front door, into the loo because like any kid I had waited too long before accepting, I really did need to 'go'. Next, into my bedroom, where I stripped off and dumped my stinking t-shirt. Then, I used my foot to kick Seema's door open as my hands were occupied pulling on a clean t-shirt that was half covering my head, half pulled out in front of me like I was some kind of skinny, Asian Stretch Armstrong. She wasn't there. So I headed towards the kitchen looking for mum and finally into the front room where the family had gathered, waiting for my return.

Dad listened to my over-excited jabbering, as always, then left the room. The reason? That bit of the story I don't remember. But the next bit I do. He came back into the living room and went absolutely nuts. Seriously, you would have thought I had dragged a dead elephant through the flat. Well, to be honest, it probably did smell as if I had because there was a stench and a trail of sticky unpleasantness everywhere.

He became a man possessed. Down came the slipper from its home on the mantelpiece. (Back then, Asian dads keeping a slipper framed above the fireplace was not an urban myth; it was a fact!) Then down it came on my skinny frame; once, twice, three times... and I will never forget the pain or the shame of that moment. It hurt, both physically and right down to the pit of my stomach. I can feel myself flinching now as if it were yesterday.

This is not leading to a declaration that I was abused as a child, far from it. I was in no doubt of the love my parents had for me. But if I did something wrong, I was punished, and for Asian dads, the slipper was the tool to teach lessons and obedience. I'm not angry with him, and he did what he thought was right at the time: what was best for me and what would encourage me to be more careful in the future. (That bit worked, as I don't think I have ever fallen foul of such a thing since.) It wasn't the first or last discipline I received from him, as I was by no means the model child, but it was by far the worst. Sadly, my dad is no longer with us, and, as I said, I do not blame him in the slightest. I know he loved me, and always did his best, but that incident has haunted me for the rest of my life.

Time with dad was always special, but he was a busy man, so he didn't get to spend a lot of one-to-one time with Seema or me. That is how it was for most working families in the late 70s, and it is still that way for many today. What has seen a decline, thankfully, is the placement of slippers on the mantelpiece. I think. But after that day, trips out with him were never quite the same. Without fail, every time we were out together, he would slap the back of my head hard and say, "Ash, look down, look down, I don't want you bringing that shit in the flat again". He would constantly and repeatedly tell me to look where I was going. Looking back, somewhere deep inside of me, even at that young age, I felt he was implying I was a fool who was destined to find trouble and spread it around for the rest of my life. And I started to believe him.

So, I learned to look down. Look down, Ash. Always. Physically and mentally, from the moment that first slipper blow hit home, I was on high alert for mess on the pavement. I can see evidence of how I began to look out for the same in life too. And to this day, I have a permanent stoop and recurring back problems, due to decades of walking with my head down, looking at the pavement.

Have you ever played 'The Pink Car' game on long journeys? If you haven't, I'm sure you will know a variation. It is the one where you look for cars the colour of snooker balls. And I always thought I was safe when it came to the pink car as not many were around when Jace was a kid (car owners are more adventurous today). But Jace was so alert and always spotted one – pretty quickly too – because that was the aim of the game. You see, when you are actively looking for something, good or bad, you are much more likely to find it. It is why the vision board exercise works so well. Because, if you fill that board with what you want to achieve, and look at it daily, you will start to see seemingly random opportunities that could help to make those things happen. It is not magic; it is simple awareness. You are looking for them, so you will be more open and receptive to prospects that lead to fulfilling the dreams and visions on your board.

My pink car was a different colour, it smelt bad, and it came with a stench and a painful reminder.

Before writing this chapter, I asked myself if I would tell that story if my dad was still alive to read it. Of course, I wouldn't, because he was totally unaware of the impact of his actions – and it would hurt him if he knew. For decades, I didn't even know myself. Dad would also be upset that his negative influence was offset a little by Peter's positive actions. Because where my dad taught me to look down and avoid trouble, Peter taught me to look up and see what the horizon could be.

I loved my dad completely, and I know that he loved me and would have done anything for Seema or me. His effort at being the best dad he could be was supreme and unquestionable. But he did affect the sort of person I became, and I would urge any parent reading this (not as an accusation but certainly as a thought) to consider the effects of what you say and do around your children. His fiery temper and anger were part of my make up too; far more than I would have liked, and it impacted in lots of ways. I would regularly throw tennis rackets across the court and scare my opponents; I was an angry teenager and carried that into my twenties. And when bad things crossed my path, I found it hard to resist stepping in with both feet.

Then one day, sometime after all the incidents I've related in the previous chapters, the barriers finally broke. I cannot remember the specific proverbial, final straw; but there I was, sitting on the psychiatrist's couch and letting the floodgates flow free. The incident with my dad, the unbearable heartbreak of losing Seema, the shame and panic of my business collapse; and realising the fragility of family love. These, plus many other failings, faux pas and the dozens of curveballs life continually throws (including the ones I was subconsciously searching out), finally took their toll. Too many double-faults, unforced errors and missed passing shots into an open court left me empty-handed.

I know I'm one of the millions who face this twentieth-century affliction and I also know the details of my story echo many others. But that is why I chose to share it. Because I hope that my story will help. Writing this and being this open has not been easy; but, as I have expressed in earlier chapters, solutions always start with being honest.

For the first time in telling this part of my story, I am going to use the word the doctor used. He said, "Ash, you are suffering from depression". Call it what you will, but what I chose to hear when he explained depression to me was that I had an injury. And in my lifetime of sporting experience, I have learned that injuries can heal, what caused the injury can be corrected, and the fault can be strengthened. Yes, accidents still happen, no matter how careful a sports person or their coaches are; but the risks can be minimised, the performance can be maximised, and the game can still be won. And here is the interesting thing about bodily injuries (to muscle and bone): your mind will often tell you that area is weak because it remembers the pain of the injury. But the reality is that the healed tissue can be much stronger than it was in the first place. Hitting walls often makes you tougher.

LESSON ONE

Life walls us in sometimes

Some walls need breaking down – whatever it takes. There really is no other way forward. And mental health is something that cannot be ignored. Just to be clear here, when I use the term 'mental health' I am not necessarily talking about the D-word or any other diagnosed condition. By definition, every single person alive today has a mental condition. Some might be described as stable, and there are medical names associated with others; but we are all on the spectrum of having a cerebral, psychological, emotional (or whatever other words you might like to use) condition of some sort. And what I have come to realise is that however people fit into that scale, we are all normal because we are all people. It is OK to struggle, it is part of being a social animal to need help, it is the cycle of life to have ups and downs, and it is perfectly normal to feel rubbish sometimes. But that doesn't mean we have to lie down and accept that we are broken. You can fight back, and you can break down the walls in front of you.

I am not against medication, and I accept there are experts out there who know how the brain and our emotions work far better than I ever will, so I will be the first to encourage anyone to take advice from professionals. In fact, that is what I did when I was given my diagnosis. The doctor gave me three choices: rest and recuperate, take pills, or start a course of therapy. Initially, I looked around to check he was talking to *me* because I wasn't ready to hear words like that; but I quickly decided I needed some coaching to get myself through this. It had worked in other areas of my life, so why not here?

In the previous chapter, I explained my belief that improvement and turning weakness into strength starts by being honest with yourself about what you want. The issue there is that those conversations are sometimes hard to have. And speaking to an independent expert or trusted friend is an easier way to reveal the truth. However you get there, you need to identify the wall that needs tackling before you can knock it down. It is no good going into a wild rage and lashing out at the world as I did for decades as a young man. That just makes things worse. Once you know what the problem is, you can take all of that destructive energy and life-changing determination, and channel it into knocking down the wall that stands in your way. And whether it is a head or heart shaped wall, the first hurdle is always the biggest – owning up and accepting the diagnosis.

So, there I was, talking to a perfect stranger (albeit one with letters after their name and an excellent couch-side manner) about the deepest darkest corners of my mind. I was amazed at how effective talking can be and taken totally by surprise at what came out. Put it this way; there are large sections of this book that I would not have been able to recall, let alone write about if it hadn't been for those sessions. Yes, there was a structure to each time we met, but for the most part, it was simply me opening up and not holding anything back. Just letting go and not being the tough one for a change. And it started to work. Over the next few weeks and months, as I continued to talk, and follow the structured rehabilitation programme (remember, I had determined that I would treat this just like a sports injury), things began to improve, and I felt better. The crucial part of the healing process, however, was that I started to understand and clearly identify the cause, and I could see there was a pathway beyond it.

On this occasion, the wall was called hopelessness. I had become walled in by the accumulation of circumstances, feelings of failure and believing that my life might be destined to be a big, misplaced, unconscious step into one unpleasant stench after another. But once I was able to identify the wall, I could focus my effort on smashing it down, and use the strength gained from my recovery exercises to do just that.

The truth is, and here is the slight chink in this particular wall analogy, that I still feel those feelings sneaking up on me from time to time. I call them my 'Black Dog' days. But mostly, I recognise the signs, and I can head off a slump before it becomes a crash. Maybe I'll heal permanently one day, or these things might always be part of me. But it doesn't matter which it is, either is OK, because I like being me again, and I've accepted that I do not have to be perfect.

LESSON TWO

Finding your natural swing

I loved teaching young people to play tennis. I don't know if it was born out of wanting to repay the faith Peter had afforded me or just the thrill of knowing I was making someone's day. But nothing gave me more of a thrill than seeing one of my students fix a fault in their backhand, hit a perfect smash, or master the technique of an overarm serve for the first time. There is something special about perfection, and that is probably why watching Roger Federer or Serena Williams play at the top of their game is so captivating. But here is the thing. They are only perfect on a good day, and because they are them.

No one on earth could learn to play tennis quite like Roger Federer. In the same way, I would never expect anyone to think, act or want in the same way as me. I can confidently say that, on my best days, I am the perfect person to do what I do. If there were a worldwide 'be Ash Taylor' competition – no one else would stand a chance. I would quite literally only have to turn up and play at 80% to be crowned the champion of the world. That is not arrogance: it is a fact (I had a tiny little dopamine rush just thinking about the idea of winning that!). And I am sure you know what is coming next: you could insert your name in that competition and revel in the same outcome. You have the potential to do incredible things. You just have to be the best version of you, playing at the top of your game, more often than not.

When I was coaching my students, I never tried to teach them the perfect swing. It does not exist. Yes, we sometimes looked at the way Agassi, Hewitt, Hingis or Davenport hit a ball or watched the senior members of the club on court, but my fundamental approach was always the same. I would watch them rally, even as an absolute beginner picking up a racket for the first time, and see what I had to work with. Moulding the person you are is always more effective than trying to be someone you are not.

If you study the working lives of all the best tennis players or any modern top-level sports person, you will notice they all have big teams around them. I don't know if there ever was a truly solo sport, but there certainly isn't such a thing now. From long-distance runners, with only their minds and the thud of their feet for company, to the Single-Handed Trans-Atlantic race competitor alone at sea for over a month. Every person who competes in a professional sport does so with a team behind them. And, the higher the level, the bigger the ambition and the greater the reward for victory; the more they invest in their team. A coaching team can include physiotherapists, data analysts, dieticians, personal trainers, psychiatrists, technical coaches, personal assistants and even stylists (as looking good on camera is all part of modern sport).

Now, I'm not suggesting you need to get that sort of team together, but you will need help if you are going to become a better version of you. You'll also notice that some of those people fill coaching roles, to help improve a person's game and performance; others look after their wellbeing, and a few are there simply to take the strain and save them time. As an example, in addition to the business team who support my work, Kay and I also employ a gardener, a cleaner and someone to wash my car. This is not because we are posh or mega wealthy; it is because we value our time together, which adds to our personal wealth.

My point is that the best you can be is the best version of you – no one else. That person is amazing, and you do not know the half of what you are capable of achieving. But while you are trying to do 'everything' in your life and reach for everyone else's levels and ideals, you do not even have an idea of the direction you should be placing your efforts. You have to slow down, stop, take time out to think and start to build a team around you. Then you can identify your strengths, manage or improve the weaknesses, and start turning your natural swing into a formidable backhand and a perfect smash.

This is the last time I am going to mention the vision board exercise. But if you haven't completed it yet, please go and do it now. And while you are there, why not write up your 'who am I?' statement.

LESSON THREE

Comparison is the thief of joy

I always thought that one of my favourite quotes, 'Comparison is the thief of joy' originated with the American author, Marianne Williamson. But a brief Google search suggests that President Theodore Roosevelt got there first. I *am* sure, however, that it was Marianne who wrote, 'Joy is what happens to us when we allow ourselves to recognise how good things really are'. I want to start this chapter with the first of those quotes and work our way towards the second.

What would be the outcome if you compared the lives of an eighteenth-century king and a twenty-first-century office worker? By 'lives' I mean things like life expectancy, health care, everyday luxuries, heating, technology, ease of travel, safety, and pretty much every fundamental human need? If you remove the size of the castle and number of servants (some of whom could very well be plotting to kill you), I think a considered view would be that 95% of the people living in the UK today have healthier and more privileged lives than the kings of centuries ago. Yet, there are people today who hate their neighbour because they drive a better car, fall into a rage because someone else got the promotion they wanted or dive into despair when their best friend gets the latest iPhone before them. I grew up in a time where there was no such thing as a smartphone, personal computers were just becoming a 'thing', and there were only four channels on the TV. Now, I realise this paragraph is a massive contradiction to the one before it – because I am making blatant comparisons – but my point is that it *is* possible to be happy without the stuff that we think will make us happy. People have been proving that for millennia. And my extension to that thought is that the desire for things we have not got is only there because we know those things exist. And we usually know they exist because people who we know (sometimes only virtually on social media) are displaying them in their perfect lives.

It is easier to set the scene for this chapter by talking about physical things, such as the latest technology and other aspirational possessions, but what I really want to bring your attention to is *you*. And I want to suggest to you that if you are unhappy with your life, maybe it is because of what you perceive other people's lives to be. When was the last time you posted on social media that your holiday was a washout, or your children failed their exams (again), or you celebrated the fact you are self-isolating for a month because of a new haircut? People only ever put good news in their feed, giving the impression that everything is always great. And most people fall into the trap of comparing themselves with those fake news, unrealistic expectations.

Go to any business networking event with a roomful of opportunity-seeking entrepreneurs, and you will see no one goes around saying they are having a really tough time of it and are desperate for your business. Some do say these things, by their actions, posture and subliminal messaging, but the actual words do not leave their lips. Almost every small business owner you meet is playing the game of pretending they are on top. Now, I'm not suggesting you start throwing your unhappiness around the room to show how honest you are. I'm simply making the point that not everything is always as it seems. I think most people know this, but we still feel compelled to compare ourselves with how we think other people are doing. There is no value in this – at all. And even if you do meet people who are running genuinely super-successful businesses and living the dream, comparing yourself with those people will not help you either. Comparison, whether it is like-for-like or against a perceived reality, will only ever leave you judging yourself. And that can never lead to happiness.

You do not need other people's permission or recognition for *you* to be happy.

I hope, by now, you have started to think about what you want your life to be. It should include a description of the lifestyle that would make you happy and how your business would need to look to support that goal. This deep and meaningful discussion with yourself will raise some practical questions for you to answer. Such as: how much money will the business need to generate for me? And: who can I get to help me, how many hours will I need to work and what new skills do I need to learn? And finally: am I prepared to face this wall and fight for the lifestyle I want?

What do you notice about all the questions above? Not a single one needs anyone else's permission. The parameters do not need to be set by anyone else and are not driven by what another business owner is doing. And the only person who can decide the size of the ambition, the level of commitment to apply and the willingness to face the wall – is you.

Joy is what happens to us when we allow ourselves to recognise how good things really are. OK – stop reading for 20 seconds, close your eyes and give yourself a happiness score (at this precise moment in time) out of ten. Now, put what happened yesterday out of your head; ignore what your neighbour is doing, forget your competitors' sales figures, and cut out thoughts of any other influences in your work life. Grab a piece of paper and write down all the things you are grateful for in your life. (I keep a dedicated notebook and do this every single day.) Then, pick up your 'who am I?' statement and read that through twice. And finally, have a quick look at your vision board. Then close your eyes again and revaluate your happiness score. Did it improve?

A final thought on comparison

Another of the triggers the psychiatrist recognised in me was how I felt guilty for wanting a happy life for *me* because my sister's life had been cut so short. This had become a subconscious barrier and may well have been another cause of my various acts of self-sabotage through the years. There are two things to learn here. Firstly, I needed to acknowledge that whether I am happy or sad, and whether I live or die, it will not bring Seema back or have even the slightest effect on what happened to her. That is a fact for everyone who carries grief or guilt from a tragedy in their past. The second point, however, is a very personal one for me. I know that if I achieve anywhere near the level of joy and fulfilment during my lifetime as she did in her short life – I will be doing well. That is not a comparison, but a beautiful aspiration and a recognition of how well she lived.

LESSON FOUR

You are what you tell yourself

On my 'Black Dog' days, I choose to write off the time completely and count it as a loss. To the best of my knowledge, no football team in any professional league in the world has ever won every single game in a season. Rocky Marciano is the only heavyweight boxing champion of the world who retired undefeated. In some sports, teams or individuals dominate for years on end: like Mercedes in Formula One, the All Blacks in Rugby or Novak Djokovic in tennis. But none of these, even at their peak, win every time they enter the arena. Sometimes you just have to write off a bad day – but that doesn't mean you have lost the war.

Having a few bad days as an individual, returning the occasional month where sales hit a low, losing money on a poor choice of employee, or getting a product launch all wrong doesn't mean you are a failure. Events in my past may have caused the days where I am not at my best, but I am no longer that person. I don't ask for my bad days to happen, but I don't give them the benefit of my time, either. I don't pretend they are not still a small part of me, but I refuse to let them define me. What you say about yourself, write down about yourself and believe about yourself goes a long way to determining who you are. And like so many of the other ideas and experiences I have shared with you in this book: the best thing is that you get to choose your definition of you.

As a little experiment, I want you to start listening to the words you use when you talk about yourself over the next few weeks. This is often quite difficult because it makes you self-conscious about the words you are using (not a bad thing in this instance): so, it is not a true reflection on how you usually speak. Perhaps you could ask someone you know and trust to listen out for you as well? Ask them to note down when you use words and phrases like these:

- I am rubbish at... (insert your usual alternative to the word 'rubbish')
- I hope that I can...
- I can't do...
- I'm such an idiot...

You might think these are just phrases or sayings that everyone uses, but I promise you, there is more to it than that. Start listening to yourself and explore how you change the way you think by changing the words you use. Remember the way your happiness score went up when you wrote down those positive outlooks earlier? Well, this is the same neuroscience at work. Simply change the words you use, and you will feel better, and when you feel better, you will see more opportunities and take more positive actions towards embracing them. Try replacing the lines above with words like these:

- I am getting better at...
- I know that I will...
- I can do...
- I am going to learn something from this...

And when the occasional dark day dawns, just accept it and see it as a day where you can switch off and rest. Perhaps that is all that bad day is telling you anyway. I have learned to recognise when a black dog's growl is around the corner, and mostly I can ward it off before it gets here. Other times, maybe if I have been pushing too hard, have taken my eye off the self-management ball, or I am slipping back into my natural urge to micromanage; I just have to lock myself in the kennel for a day (sometimes two). But I don't beat myself up on those days anymore, I never mention it, and it doesn't go in the diary. It was just one of those unimportant statistical blips that will get forgotten in the records as my team marches on towards a winning season.

LESSON FIVE

Try something new: I dare you

In this book, I have shared real examples of significant walls I have faced in my life. There have been good walls and bad ones; actual walls and walls I have used as analogies; walls that represented challenges to traverse and those that just needed to be smashed down. I hope that as you have read my stories, you have identified some of your own. And that some of the thoughts and strengths I have shared have encouraged you to use or deal with the walls in your life. I pride myself on being a realist, and I am very conscious that some of the things I have talked about may seem a bit 'woo-woo' to a few readers. Things like positive affirmations, vision boards and keeping a gratitude diary might seem a little new-age for serious business owners, I know. And even the idea of opening up about weaknesses, talking about feelings or getting professional help might go against the grain for some. As I have mentioned throughout this book, I didn't always see things the way I do now. So I understand if you feel that way at first.

For me, it took the death of a beloved sister, the threat from an ignored child, losing a £300k business and a few hours on a psychiatrist's couch, before I stopped banging my head against the proverbial brick wall and tried something new. The person who says 'I can't' never tries anything. While those who decide they have nothing to lose might fail once or twice (or many times); but at least they get to find out if there was an answer there. The same approach can be applied to some of the more traditional and practical ideas I have put forward about business building. But even then, it takes some bold thinking and openness to new ideas to approach the process of building, trusting and managing a team in quite the way I have described. To fully hand over everything that someone else could do better than you, or you could pay them less than you do yourself, takes real strength of character. Especially if you have got the time to do it yourself or your budget is tight.

To take action on most of the things I've talked about in this book starts with you understanding yourself better and recognising your true worth. And that includes the commercial value of your expertise, what your time is worth, how you want to use the time you have each day, and having absolute clarity around what you want your life to be.

So, I dare you to go and try something new.

When I was coaching my tennis students, there would always be one or two things with each player that were a stumbling block to them. It might be that they feared looking silly if they missed a smash, so they always let the ball bounce first and in doing so lost the opportunity to win the point with one glorious shot. Or perhaps they didn't have the confidence to go for the cheeky, but ever-so-effective drop shot because it upset opponents. The point is that you do not have to master these sorts of shots to win tennis matches – and you might only get a handful of opportunities to execute them in a match anyway. But having them up your sleeve might just give you that edge in pressure situations, or win you a key point, or make your opponent a little bit wary of what you might do next. So, you are missing out on a potentially match-winning skill if you choose to ignore them. These are not easy shots to perfect, and even the pros struggle sometimes.

The fear of trying is usually born out of previous failure. Maybe the difficulty of the shot or having looked silly in front of a crowd. So, my conversations with students about their no-go shots would start like this. First, I go through the points I mentioned above, suggesting the advantages that being able to pull off these shots might add to their game. My aim would always be to show them their fears were based on a possible outcome, not the actual shot itself. And from that point, I asked if they could accept that they 'might' succeed if they tried. I would then ask for their permission to try something new.

The agreement was simply that they would try the shot, at least once, during their next match. It didn't always work, and sometimes I had to go through the entire process a few times, but for most players, they eventually realised they could become better at a new skill if they tried. There was a risk of hitting a wall, yes, but the alternative was guaranteed to stop their advance. So the odds were always in favour of trying.

Based on that philosophy, as we turn over the page and enter the final chapter of this book, I challenge you to be brave and try something new.

LESSON SIX

Turning points...

It was 26th May 1999, the end of an incredible season for the most famous football club in the world. (Even as I write this, it pains me, because I am far from being a Manchester United fan). The club needed to win one more game to land a famous treble, but the formidable Bayern Munich stood in their way in that year's Champions League Final: and, after scoring early, in the sixth minute, they put on a typical masterclass of resilience and confidence. No one could doubt the Red Devils' passionate will and determination to get back into the game, from start to finish, but it looked like they were never going to break through. If you watched the game, I am sure you will remember the drama and excitement of what happened next. And even if you do not remember that famous night, or even care, I am sure you can guess how the story ends. That is right. As the game drifted past the regulation ninety minutes and into just three minutes of injury time, Manchester United's efforts finally paid off. And in a flurry of heart-stopping action, they scored twice in quick succession through Teddy Sheringham and then Ole Gunnar Solskjær. It was an adrenaline-pumping spectacle, and I have to admit to jumping up and down with glee as the team that most English football fans love to hate pulled off an improbable comeback.

But here is the thing. What most people forget is that a few minutes before the first of those game-changing goals went in, the German team had hit the United crossbar with an overhead kick that looked destined to seal their victory. And, watching the reaction of the team in red, in the seconds that followed that stroke of good fortune, I believe that moment was the true turning point.

We always remember victories in our lives, and we spend much of our time dreaming of future ambitions; places we are going to go, things we want to do and the wealth we are going to create. Most of the business owners I know, in fact, most of the *people* I know, are either fighting demons from their past or daydreaming about an unlikely future. And because their focus (head, heart and vision) is in their past or future, they are left battling away blindly at the walls around them now. Yet that is the time and place where their effort will actually make any difference—the present.

As an avid watcher of sport, I find myself looking for the turning points all the time. I do not always get it right (don't call me for racing tips), but it is surprising how often you can sense changes in the atmosphere, stance or flow of a game – just before the score begins to reverse. It is that 'we are going to score in a minute' feeling or the twitch in Sir Mo Farah's stride as he is about to pull through the crowd. It might be a missed catch in the slips, an opponent's double-fault, a lucky bounce taking a ball onto the green, a boxer on the ropes surviving a flurry of punches, or even watching a competitor take a deep breath as you almost hear their inner voice say 'I can do this.' It is these key turning points that lead to victory – not scoring the goal itself.

The problem with waiting for good things to happen is that they rarely happen on their own. Sometimes good luck does come our way. I talked earlier about how I met Kay, totally by chance a hundred miles from where I was supposed to be that weekend. I was in a dark place then and had every human right to have my eyes closed or looking down. The turning point only happened because I was awake to the moment despite my circumstances. Unless you are on the lookout for those fortunate turning points or opportunities in the present day, you might miss them. The other alternative is to step up and make them happen yourself. But again, you can only do that today. You can choose to make today a turning point in your life, and business, by looking at what you have and what you want; then taking positive action towards making it happen.

Final thought on hitting the wall

Peter Hennessy Smith taught me to look up and open the door to what was possible. He was passionate about tennis, creating opportunities for young people, coaching and improving people's game and spreading his love for the sport. What he did rubbed off on me and influenced my entire life. As I moved on and started chasing those dreams, other events and circumstances came my way. Some were good, others were cruel, many were of my own making, and more were thrust upon me. I acted and reacted in various ways; sometimes with better judgement than at other times, and eventually, the person who is writing this book came out at the other end.

I hope I have many years to come, but I can honestly say that today, I like who I am. I can look in the mirror, and I am proud of me for having made it this far (largely intact). I know there are sadder and tougher stories out in the world than mine, but all I can do is make the most of the hand I was dealt, play my best game, and be grateful for the cards I have been fortunate enough to pull from the pack.

If that brief description of my life, to date, sounds like it is the result of luck more than process or you think I am suggesting life is a whirlwind of chance where the fortunate win and the wretched are doomed to fail, think again. The fact is, everyone alive is the result of a trillions-to-one chance of nature. What you do with that chance is up to you. Gary Player was right, the more you practise, the luckier you get.

One, two, three, four, miss... "It's OK Ash, try again." One, two, three, four, five...

CLOSING THOUGHTS

Playing the game of business is an exciting and challenging rollercoaster ride, and I am in awe of those who take that leap of faith; backing themselves to give value to the wider community and the world.

Nothing gives me as much joy as seeing people achieving success on their terms. Or when they overcome adversity – often with a tenacity bordering on ferociousness! It has been a pleasure to help many business owners on their journeys and, whether you are providing a service, selling a product or developing new technology; the grit, determination, and persistence involved is something to be shouted about and applauded. You should feel proud.

Hitting the Wall was never intended to be a manual or bible – it is a guide. A story you can take heart from and lessons you can learn if you choose to. I know that resources are something to be cherished and used as often as possible. Without a doubt, my business experience has been added to by brilliant coaches, mentors, books and research.

So, never be afraid to ask for support because there are people out there with a wealth of experience, and they are willing to share. All you have to do is be aware that you need help, then ask for it.

Many people have been where you are. They have made mistakes, but they have also achieved great things. All of this is knowledge, and 'intel' is worth tapping into. Who knows? There may be your own Peter Hennessey Smith around the corner, waiting to support, advise, challenge and guide someone like you.

NEXT STEPS

I hope you've enjoyed reading this book as much as I have enjoyed writing it.

I also hope that even if you've taken only one thing from it, you are using that one thing to make a positive difference in your life. Please let me know if you have, I would genuinely love to know. And if you could leave a review on Amazon so more people can make an informed decision about whether to purchase Hitting the Wall, that would be amazing.

And, as a thank you gift for taking the time to read this, I would like to offer you a complimentary membership to The Business Clubhouse for one month. That's as long as it should take for you to see it's a community full of inspiring business owners, just like you. Collaborating and learning together to grow their businesses and improve their lives.

You can also join us on Facebook at The Business Clubhouse Forum where you'll be able to share your business experiences; ask questions; find answers: and get involved in discussions about general business strategy in a supportive environment. Or, you can reach out and email us at: **hello@thebusinessclubhouse.co.uk**

Many are playing against their own walls – but the point is, they're not playing alone. And nor should you. So please, do join us...

www.thebusinessclubhouse.co.uk

THE AUTHOR

After a prosperous career as an LTA tennis coach and owner of an award-winning business, Ash Taylor now uses those experiences to influence and inform his career as a professional business coach and motivational speaker.

Ash has worked with over 130 businesses, delivering more than 42,000 thousand hours of coaching time with many of his clients choosing to stay with him long-term so he can continue to support, encourage and mentor change in their businesses.

He remains close to his roots and works with young people as a committed Enterprise Advisor for his local Secondary School; supporting, inspiring and connecting students to the local business community.

Ash founded and runs The Business Clubhouse, a place where business owners come to improve their game. He is passionate about building a community where those business owners can access first-class support, coaching and mentoring; and be able to say they too have found their dream life.

Ash is a devoted husband and father. And, it cannot go unmentioned that he is a lifelong QPR supporter! But also an avid golfer, and all-round sports fan.

Through everything, his biggest influence is, and always will be, his little sister, Seema.

ACKNOWLEDGEMENTS

The Players

Several people have played this game of business with me over the years: all of them influencing and guiding me. Some of them knew it, some not. Either way, winning needs teamwork – and I couldn't have done any of it without you.

Warm-up	Peter Henesey Smith for setting me on this path
First Set	Martin Norbury for helping me find a way forward when I was lost
Second Set	Terry Gormley, Chris Waters, Gary Drake and Dan Harrison for stepping up when I needed it
Third Set	Pieter De Villiers for rare steak, red wine, and single malt
Fourth Set	Gary Fullwood, the strongest man I know
Fifth Set	James Welsh and John Thompson, there can never be enough golf in the sun
Cool Down	Martin Gladdish, thank you for bringing this story to life

Erol, Des, Shane, Michael, Miguel – being able to count your friends on one hand is a blessing if they're the right friends; and you are.

To my amazing TBC team: Hannah, Theresa, Shirley and of course, Chrystel at Plum Design & Publishing. This would never have seen the light of day without your continuous support. I'm forever grateful that you've taken it upon yourselves to share the role of being either alongside me as friends, behind me to push when I've needed it, and in front of me to pull (often!).

And finally, all our members, past and present who make this journey such a blast.

Your trust in me is humbling.

Ash

Printed in Great Britain
by Amazon

67196218R00078